SpringerBriefs in Economics

SpringerBriefs present concise summaries of cutting-edge research and practical applications across a wide spectrum of fields. Featuring compact volumes of 50 to 125 pages, the series covers a range of content from professional to academic. Typical topics might include:

- A timely report of state-of-the art analytical techniques
- A bridge between new research results, as published in journal articles, and a contextual literature review
- A snapshot of a hot or emerging topic
- An in-depth case study or clinical example
- A presentation of core concepts that students must understand in order to make independent contributions

SpringerBriefs in Economics showcase emerging theory, empirical research, and practical application in microeconomics, macroeconomics, economic policy, public finance, econometrics, regional science, and related fields, from a global author community.
Briefs are characterized by fast, global electronic dissemination, standard publishing contracts, standardized manuscript preparation and formatting guidelines, and expedited production schedules.

Gianluca Biggi

Industrial Dynamics and Firm Strategies in the Agrochemical Industry

Springer

Gianluca Biggi
Institute of Economics
Scuola Superiore Sant'Anna
Pisa, Italy

ISSN 2191-5504 ISSN 2191-5512 (electronic)
SpringerBriefs in Economics
ISBN 978-3-031-52688-6 ISBN 978-3-031-52689-3 (eBook)
https://doi.org/10.1007/978-3-031-52689-3

This Springer imprint is published by the registered company Springer Nature Switzerland AG
The registered company address is: Gewerbestrasse 11, 6330 Cham, Switzerland

Paper in this product is recyclable.

Preface

Industrialized economies have historically maintained the hope that the advances in science, technology and innovation would have offered to humanity a wide range of options to improve its well-being and attain sustained economic growth. The transition towards a high technological frontier arising from the rapid advances of science, technology and innovation has opened a debate on the relations between innovation-induced industrial activities, related possible social and environmental threats like climate change, resource depletion and emerging pollution-driven health crises, and the role of regulation and government intervention to keep up with industry developments. While the potential of regulation and government intervention to shape firms' innovative behaviour and related R&D activities towards socially desirable and environmentally acceptable outcomes has been widely acknowledged, the impact of regulations on potentially harmful technologies or innovations are produced is not well understood.

Our knowledge on the impacts of environmental regulations on potentially harmful products, processes or technologies is scant, which creates opportunities for research especially as environmental hazards and risks are currently receiving heightened media and policy attention. While pesticides like DDT or PBC appear to be a menace from the past, new chemical compounds are currently receiving considerable attention for their potential hazardous impacts. A case in point is glyphosate, a herbicide currently used especially in connection with genetically modified crops, which the WHO Agency for Research on Cancer (IARC) classified it as 'probably carcinogenic' in 2015 after numerous independent studies provided evidence of its connection to the emergence of different forms of cancers. Like glyphosate there are many other harmful innovations, or otherwise defined 'contested technologies', that are still in use despite evidence of their hazardous impacts on humans and the ecosystem. In a recent article, Alex Coad, Gianluca Biggi and Elisa Giuliani show that contested technologies sometimes take decades to be banned, which creates enough opportunity space for firms to extend the exploitation of their existing technologies, especially in loosely regulated countries, and despite their well-known hazards.

Because of this lag and uncertainty regarding the ban of hazardous innovations, it seems timely to investigate the potential hazards enshrined in companies' inventive phase. Knowing the potential toxicity of ongoing inventions can help anticipate future hazards. In contemporary society, we are chronically exposed to a mixture of chemicals, which, even at low doses, can be toxic for human health and the environment. In this context, I ask: what are companies doing in their R&D labs: are their inventions less toxic (and potentially less hazardous) over time? Are current environmental regulations effective in curbing corporate inventions of harmful products?

From an evolutionary economics' perspective, firms can search for technical novelty both by exploring new technological spaces and/or exploiting prior knowledge. The balance depends on the relative costs of exploration and exploitation and the ability to apply prior expertise towards future paths. Explorative search is costly and risky, and the balance depends on the relative cost of exploration and exploitation. The idea of induced innovation recognizes that R&D is a profit-motivated investment activity, and that the direction of innovation likely corresponds positively to the direction of increased relative cost.

Environmental regulation can spur explorative search reducing its relative cost. Some scholars indicate that environmental regulation can spur firms' ability to innovate, by lowering its relative cost of exploration. That regulation can help direct towards new combinations of products or processes. Thus, environmental regulation is theorized as allowing firms to enlarge their innovative outcomes. In the chemical sector, environmental regulation can trigger the transformation process of existing chemical compounds and substances. In that context, my hypotheses suggest that, after a ban, companies and other inventing entities will take new 'explorative' innovation paths and therefore will make new knowledge around the regulated technologies. They also will potentially explore radically new technological trajectories. My results show that after a global ban to regulate POPs' use, production and trade, the number of new firms inventing around POP-related technologies, as well as a global spread of POP-related patent applications in developing countries, increased (Chap. 1). I also find that environmental regulation had a significant effect on the number of patented compounds as well as in the number of newly invented compounds (Chap. 2). Finally, building on computational chemistry techniques, I introduce novel indicators for the toxicity prediction of chemical inventions by analysing POP-related technologies with a control group of unregulated technologies (Chap. 3).

Methodologically, my book is original for the following reasons. First, I build for the first time a dataset that combines patent data with chemical structures data. The approach follows extant methodologies but my focus is more narrow on chemical compounds' patent claims which allows me to identify more neatly the innovative space for which companies seek intellectual property rights (IPR) protection.

Second, I combine patent analysis with computational chemistry and toxicology, which is unprecedented in innovation and management studies (the research methodology used here has been published by Gianluca Biggi and co-authors in an international peer-reviewed article in 2021). Computational chemistry is a chemistry branch which, combined with toxicology, uses mathematical algorithms, statistics and large databases to analyse and experiment chemical substances and related toxicological properties.

Finally, this book's work represents one of the first steps to uncover R&D lab activities and assess their potential hazards for humans and the environment, which has potentially significant implications on public policy, R&D management and firm strategy.

Pisa, Italy
November 2023

Gianluca Biggi

Ethics Approval This book does not report research involving human or animal participant, so no ethics approval is required.

Competing Interests The author declared no potential conflicts of interest with respect to the research, authorship and/or publication of this book.

Many the wonders but nothing more wondrous than man.
This thing crosses the sea in the winter's storm,
making his path through the roaring waves.
And she, the greatest of gods, the Earth-
deathless she is, and unwearied-he wears her away
as the ploughs go up and down from year
to year and his mules tum up the soil.
The tribes of the light hearted birds he ensnares, and the races
of all the wild beasts and the salty brood of the sea,
with the twisted mesh of his nets, he leads captive, this clever man.
He controls with craft the beasts of the open air,
who roams the hills. The horse with his shaggy mane
he holds and harnesses, yoked about the neck,
and the strong bull of the mountain.
Speech and thought like the wind.
and the feelings that make the town,
he has taught himself, and shelter against the cold,
refuge from rain. Ever resourceful is he.
He faces no future helpless. Only against death
shall he call for aid in vain. But from baffling maladies
has he contrived escape.
Clever beyond all dreams
the inventive craft that he has
which may drive him one time or another to well or ill.
When he honours the laws of the land and the gods' sworn right
high indeed is his city; but stateless the man
who dares to do what is shameful.

Sophocles, Antigone, c. 441 B.C. (332–369)

Acknowledgments

I extend my sincere gratitude to Elisa Giuliani and Arianna Martinelli for their invaluable research advice, supervision and insightful comments throughout the Ph.D. journey. I am also indebted to Stefan Wagner, Nate Niu Jingze, Emilio Benfenati, Stefania Giannarelli, Tiziano Tuccinardi, Giulio Poli, Andrea Pucci, Julio Raffo, Lorena Rivera Leon, Gabriel Berlicki and Daly Alica for their excellent research guidance. I express my appreciation to two anonymous referees whose comments were instrumental in enhancing the quality of this book. Additionally, I would like to thank the participants and attendees of the 18th Annual Conference of the European Policy for Intellectual Property Protection (EPIP 2023) in Krakow, Poland, in September 2023; the DRUID Conference 2023 in Lisbon, Portugal, in June 2023; the 6th Geography of Innovation Conference (GEOINNO2022) in Milan, Italy, in July 2022; the 6th Global Conference on Economic Geography (GCEG Dublin 2022) in Dublin, Ireland, in June 2022; the Summer School for Data and Algorithms on ST&I Studies in Leuven, Belgium, in September 2020; the ETH Academy on Sustainability and Technology in Zürich, Switzerland, in June 2019; the 80th Annual Meeting of the Academy of Management (AOM) in Vancouver, Canada, in August 2020; the 26th Annual SPRU PhD Forum in Brighton, UK, in May 2020; the 5th Geography of Innovation Conference (GEOINNO2020) in Stavanger, Norway, in January 2020; and the 79th Annual Meeting of the Academy of Management (AOM) in Boston, USA, in August 2019. As always, I acknowledge the standard disclaimers.

About This Book

This book is about the extent and modalities in which companies react to regulations in their innovative activities. We live in a world of sustainability challenges not just because of climate change. There are other major environmental degradation problems that are as important as global warming and deserve scholarly and policy attention. This book explores companies' innovative strategies and, more specifically, their inventive patterns in one specific context: that of pesticides and other potentially toxic chemicals. This is an area that deserves attention because of the growing scientific evidence about the link between human exposure to certain chemicals and the emergence of several illnesses of our times (such as cancer and neurodegenerative diseases). For this reason, one of the EU Green Deal's goal is the promotion of a toxic-free environment for the future.

In this book, I focus on a specific category of hazardous chemical innovations, known as Persistent Organic Pollutants (POPs). I focus on this specific class of toxic products because they are amongst the most dangerous chemicals ever invented – and their dangers stand in their high toxicity, persistency in the environment and body and the fact that they travel long distance. POPs have been widely used in agriculture especially after the World War II in developed countries, but their use has spread considerably during the last decades in developing countries.

The Book Is Composed of Three Chapters

- **Chapter 1**: 'Geographical and Industrial Dynamics of Chemical Inventions: The Case of Persistent Organic Pollutants'

  Abstract: Persistent organic pollutants (POPs) are a class of highly toxic chemical substances, and for this reason, their use, production, and trade have been banned across countries worldwide. I examine the first group of POPs to be banned (i.e., aldrin, chlordane, dieldrin, endrin, heptachlor, hexachlorobenzene, mirex, polychlorinated biphenyls (PCBs), toxaphene, DDT, pentachlorobenzene and polychlorinated dibenzo-p-dioxins) and investigate the historical and emergent pattern of POP-related inventions by way of a unique dataset that includes patent applications over the period 1991–2010. I find an industry growth over time characterized by an increasing number of new firms inventing around POP-related technologies as well as a diffusion in a range of new countries such as China, Argentina, Brazil and Russia rather than the USA, EU and Japan where POP-related inventions were first filed in history.

- **Chapter 2**: 'Assessing Policy Impact on Organizational Inventions: The Case of the Stockholm Convention'
  Abstract: Once companies develop hazardous products which can be dangerous for the environment and human health, it takes very long for regulatory bodies to ban these products. However, very little is known about the impact of regulatory action on firms' inventive strategies. Using a difference-in-difference approach, I test the impact of regulation on a sample of POP-related patents against a control sample of untreated pesticides. Interestingly, I find that the signature and/or ratification of Stockholm Convention – the UN ban on the use, trade and production of persistent organic pollutants – increases the rate of POP-related invention and new compound patenting, opening up interesting questions about corporate innovative strategies and calling for further research on the nature of the new POP-related inventions.
- **Chapter 3**: 'Are We Moving Towards a More Sustainable World? Insights from Patent Analysis of Chemical Inventions'

  Abstract: Industrialized economies have historically maintained the hope that the advances in science, technology and innovation would have offered to humanity a wide range of options to improve its well-being and attain sustained economic growth. The transition towards a high technological frontier arising from the rapid advances of science, technology and innovation has opened a debate on the relations between innovation-induced industrial activities, related possible social and environmental threats and the role of policies to keep up with industry developments. To investigate those relations, I collect a unique dataset that includes patent applications in chemical technologies and analyse their disclosed groups of compounds by combining patent analysis with computational chemistry, and I develop a novel methodology to measure patent toxicity, that is, the extent to which a patent includes 'components' (i.e. chemical compounds) that are potentially toxic to humans and/or the environment. To illustrate the proposed methodology, I analyse the toxicity of 12 regulated chemical technologies as the persistent organic pollutants (POPs) in comparison with a control group of unregulated technologies. The measurement of patent toxicity opens up interesting avenues for future research and for policy.

Contents

About the Author

Gianluca Biggi is currently a postdoctoral researcher at the Institute of Economics at the Sant'Anna School of Advanced Studies in Pisa. He completed his Ph.D. in Management at the University of Pisa in 2021. In 2023, he was visiting researcher at the European School of Management and Technology (ESMT) Berlin. In 2020, he was a visiting researcher at the Department of Science and Technology Studies at University College London (UCL), and in June 2018, he was a visiting researcher at the Sloan School of Management at MIT. His research focuses on exploring the nature and dynamics of innovation. During his Ph.D., he contributed to the development of a new methodology that combines the extraction of chemical content from patents with computational chemistry techniques to understand the nature of chemical inventions.

He has received the following recognition:

Industry and Innovation: Inclusion of the article "The Noxious Consequences of Innovation: What do we know?" in the collection of the top 30 impact research articles published in the journal to date (April 2023).
DRUID Conference 2023: Nomination for the Best Paper Award by Industry and Innovation (January 2023).
AREA Science Park: Award for the best Ph.D. thesis utilizing intellectual property rights (IPR) (January 2022).
Academy of International Business (AIB): Nomination for the AIB-Aalto "That's Interesting Award!" (May 2020).

Chapter 1
Geographical and Industrial Dynamics of Chemical Inventions: The Case of Persistent Organic Pollutants

Abstract Persistent organic pollutants (POPs) are a class of highly toxic chemical substances, and for this reason, their use, production, and trade have been banned across countries worldwide. I examine the first group of POPs to be banned (i.e., aldrin, chlordane, dieldrin, endrin, heptachlor, hexachlorobenzene, mirex, polychlorinated biphenyls (PCBs), toxaphene, DDT, pentachlorobenzene and polychlorinated dibenzo-p-dioxins) and investigate the historical and emergent pattern of POP-related inventions by way of a unique dataset that includes patent applications over the period 1991–2010. I find an industry growth over time characterized by an increasing number of new firms inventing around POP-related technologies as well as a diffusion in a range of new countries such as China, Argentina, Brazil and Russia rather than the USA, EU and Japan where POP-related inventions were first filed in history.

1.1 Introduction

Regulation and government intervention have the potential to shape firms' innovative behaviour and related R&D activities toward desirable economic, social and environmental goals or to divert it. Despite the extraordinary economic and social progresses reaped over the last decades through technological changes and innovation, the protection of human health and natural ecosystems persists as global challenges (Meadows et al. 2004; Steffen et al. 2016) and firms – as the main locus of innovation – play a major role in the process of sustainable development. As a consequence, economists and management scholars have increasingly paid attention to the relations between policy, technology and organizations in relation to sustainable development. These relations have been traditionally investigated by looking at technology and innovation as a clear-cut engine of economic growth and prosperity. Against this background, scholarly and policy attention has been directed on how to align social and environmental goals with technology and innovation objectives to achieve a 'sustainable' and 'inclusive' growth at firm, industry and national level

G. Biggi, *Industrial Dynamics and Firm Strategies in the Agrochemical Industry*, SpringerBriefs in Economics, https://doi.org/10.1007/978-3-031-52689-3_1

(Schot and Steinmueller 2018). The most recent policy initiatives witnessed such rationale as in the case of supranational environmental regulations of the United Nations Environment Programme (UNEP), the UN Sustainable Development Goals (SDGs) as well as the Responsible Research and Innovation (RRI) funding programme of the EU Horizon 2020.

Therefore, while most extant research either in management studies or broader economics literature have been very sophisticated in investigating and measuring the drivers and consequences of sustainability-oriented growth at different levels, few studies of technological change and innovation address directly the noxious consequences of innovation (for a review see Biggi and Giuliani (2020)). I argue that the investigation of the noxious consequences of innovation-induced industrial activities plays a pivotal role in understanding the interplay between policies and firms' innovative activities in relation to sustainable development processes.

In this chapter, I collect a unique dataset that includes patent applications in chemical technologies, and I examine historical and emergent patterns of the R&D-related activities behind those technologies. My data covers all the patent applications claiming the 12 hazardous technologies universally recognized as causing adverse effects on human and ecosystems by the UN Stockholm Convention on Persistent Organic Pollutants (hereinafter POPs) (namely, aldrin, chlordane, dieldrin, endrin, heptachlor, hexachlorobenzene, mirex, polychlorinated biphenyls (PCBs), toxaphene, DDT, pentachlorobenzene and polychlorinated dibenzo-p-dioxins (PCDD/F)).

Despite the known drawbacks of patents as a measure of innovation (i.e., they are a measure of invention independent on whether it makes it into the final market and not all innovations are patented), patent data are widely accepted and employed to proxy innovative activities (Griliches 1990; Hall et al. 2001; Hall and Haroff 2012). Furthermore, scholars have been very active in developing patent indicators to highlight different characteristics of the disclosed innovation. For instance, as patent documents do not have any direct indication of the value of the disclosed inventions, some 'indirect' measures such as patent citations (Trajtenberg 1990; Hall and Martin 2005; Harhoff et al. 1999), patent renewals (Schankerman and Pakes 1985), and patent families (Lanjouw et al. 1998; Harhoff et al. 2003) have been developed and validated to know more about their characteristics and qualities. Patent claims and the number of IPC classes have been used to measure the scope of the patents both from the technological (Lerner 1994) and legal point of views (Lanjouw et al. 1998; Lanjouw and Schankerman 2001; Kuhn and Thompson 2017). Still, information about the technological dispersion of both forward and backward citations (i.e., the citation received and made, respectively) have been combined in indicators of patent generality and originality (Jaffe and de Rassenfosse 2017). These measures are used extensively in academic research, especially in economics and related fields, to understand the drivers and consequences of economic growth in relation to sustainable development processes.

1.2 Methods

1.2.1 The Patent Databases

In this study, I rely on two main databases: the chemical database of the European Molecular Biology Laboratory (SureChEMBL) and the EPO-PATSTAT. SureChEMBL is a publicly available large-scale database (Papadatos et al. 2016) which has the unique feature of providing comprehensive compound-patent association maps and includes information indicating the chemical compounds extracted from a specific section of a specific patent document such as the title, abstract, claims or the patent text. The SureChEMBL database provides also information on chemical compound international identifiers (i.e., ChEMBL identifier, SMILES, standard InChIKey) that allow to precisely search all the patents related to a specific compound. To retrieve all the patents associated with each POP, I use one or multiple CAS Registry Number identifiers (see Table 1.1 for the details of the search strategy).[1] Most importantly, the ChEMBL database allows us to identify all patents that cite a POP in its claims, which are the extent (i.e., the scope) of the protection sought in a patent application (Kuhn and Thompson 2019; Bekkers et al. 2020; Marco et al. 2019; Jayaraj and Gittelman 2018).

The search in SureChEMBL identifies 1113 POP-related patent applications at European Patent Office (EPO), US Patent Office (USPTO), Japan Patent Office (JPO), and World Intellectual Property Organization (WIPO) between 1990 and 2010. I decided to focus on patent applications because they give a window onto the exploratory efforts of assignees, unlike granted patents, which only represent a small percentage of the filed applications. Some of the retrieved patent applications might protect the same invention in multiple legislations among the four available in the SureChEMBL database. To avoid double or multiple counts, I focus the analysis at the unique DOCDB patent family level.[2] I then use the EPO-PATSTAT (version Autumn 2018) database to identify the DOCDB patent families for all the POP-related patent applications retrieved from the SureChEMBL database. The final set includes 624 unique DOCDB patent families including 5240 patent applications filed in 75 patent authorities of which 233 (2.52%) related to aldrin, 840 (9.08%) related to chlordane, 1044 (11.29%) related to dieldrin, 1072 (11.59%) related to endrin, 759 (8.21%) related to heptachlor, 2348 (25.39%) related to

[1]A CAS Registry Number is a unique numerical identifier assigned by the Chemical Abstracts Service (CAS) to every chemical substance described in the open scientific literature including organic and inorganic compounds.

[2]A patent family is defined as a set of patents taken in various countries to protect a single invention. Depending on some technicalities of patent application procedures worldwide and the definition of the so-called patent priorities, there are several definitions of patent family (e.g. 'simple' patent families vs. 'extended' patent families). In this chapter, I adopt a conservative approach using the DOCDB family. This is considered one of the most restrictive 'simple' patent families that ensures that only patents covering the same invention are included in the family (see Martínez 2011 for a discussion).

Table 1.1 Sampling strategy

Chemical	CAS registry number	Molecular formula	SureChEMBL identifier
Aldrin	309-00-2	C12 H8 Cl6	SCHEMBL119263
Chlordane	57-74-9	C10 H6 Cl8	SCHEMBL75811
Dieldrin	60-57-1	C12 H8 Cl6 O	SCHEMBL72829
Endrin	72-20-8	C12 H8 Cl6 O	SCHEMBL72828
Heptachlor	76-44-8	C10 H5 Cl7	SCHEMBL65124
Hexachlorobenzene	118-74-1	C6 Cl6	SCHEMBL26562
Mirex	2385-85-5	C10 Cl12	SCHEMBL118586
Polychlorinated biphenyls (PCBs)	Main 1336-36-3	C12H10−xClx	SCHEMBL2906064
Toxaphene	8001-35-2	C10 H10 Cl8	SCHEMBL5933656
DDT	50-29-3	C14 H9 Cl5	SCHEMBL7181
Pentachlorobenzene	608-93-5	C6 H Cl5	SCHEMBL183144
Polychlorinated dibenzo-p-dioxins and furans (PCDDs/ PCDDFs)	Multiple: 1746-01-6; 40321-76-4; 39227-28-6; 57653-85-7; 19408-74-3; 35822-46-9; 3268-87-9; 51207-31-9; 57117-41-6; 57117-31-4; 70648-26-9; 57117-44-9; 72918-21-9; 60851-34-5; 67562-39-4; 55673-89-7; 39001-02-0	Multiple: C12 H4 Cl4 O2; C12 H3 Cl5 O2; C12 H2 Cl6 O2; C12 H2 Cl6 O2; C12 H2 Cl6 O2; C12 H Cl7 O2; C12 Cl8 O2; C12 H4 Cl4 O; C12 H3 Cl5 O; C12 H3 Cl5 O; C12 H2 Cl6 O; C12 H2 Cl6 O; C12 H2 Cl6 O; C12 H2 Cl6 O; C12 H Cl7 O; C12 H Cl7 O; C12 Cl8 O	SCHEMBL8939; SCHEMBL4170319; SCHEMBL1954279

Source: Author's own elaboration

hexachlorobenzene, 328 (3.55%) related to mirex, 29 (0.31%) related to polychlorinated biphenyls (PCBs), 801 (8.66%) related to DDT, 30 (0.32%) related to pentachlorobenzene, and 624 (19.07%) related to polychlorinated dibenzo-p-dioxins.

Of the 5240 retrieved patent applications, 834 (15.92%) have the filing of the first patent application at the USPTO, 721 (13.76%) to the EPO, and 373 (7.12%) to the JPO. Over the period of observations, the assignee patent applications are in the majority companies (6966; 91.26%), followed by individual inventors (376; 4.93%) and universities or public research organizations (291; 3.81%). To enlarge the analysis to the global level, I retrieve all the family members for all the 624 unique DOCDB families from the PATSTAT database. This information allows tracing all the legislations in which POP-related patents are filed. The final dataset thus includes 624 unique DOCDB patent families which represent 5240 individual patent applications covering 75 countries.

1.3 Empirical Results

1.3.1 Temporal Patterns

In this section, I consider the overall trends of POP-related inventions. To this end, I use the 5240 unique patent applications to depict the distribution of inventive efforts and their temporal pattern. I am interested in understanding POP-related patent applications prior and after the environmental regulation (i.e. the Stockholm Convention). To this end, I consider both 2001 and 2004 as key years: the former corresponds to the year in which the convention was signed by a total of 91 countries worldwide, while the latter corresponds to the Convention entering into force when 128 countries have ratified the convention to eliminate or restrict the production and use of POPs. Figure 1.1 shows the count of POP-related patent applications filed each year over the period 1990–2010. On an aggregate basis, I observe a steep increase in POP-related inventions after 2001 even though at a variable rate.

Table 1.2 reports the number of DOCDB family applications for each POP, before and after 2001. Dieldrin and mirex are the technologies with a higher average annual growth rate for the two periods; this means that they grew more than the total in every period. Additionally, after 2001, aldrin and pentachlorobenzene show the highest rates of growth indicating innovative efforts behind those technologies.

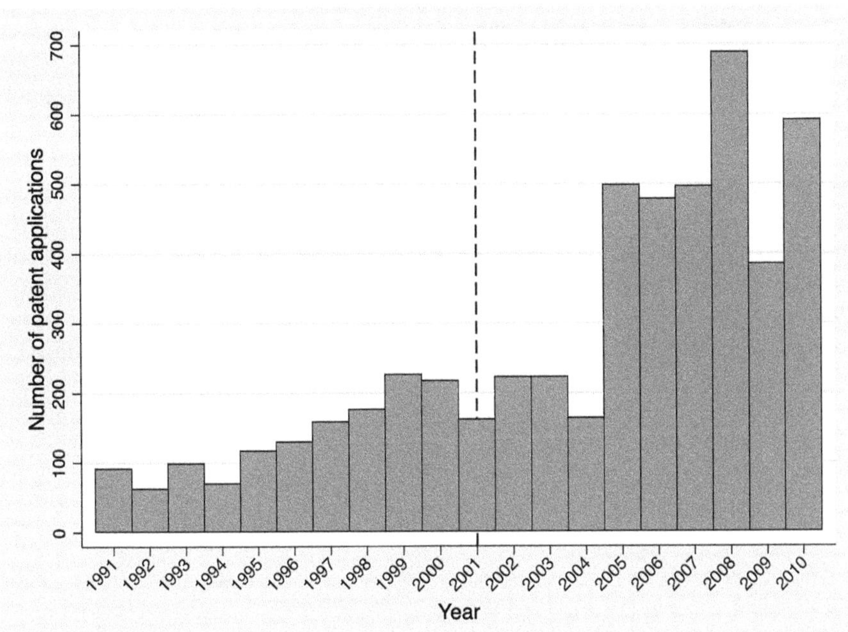

Fig. 1.1 Evolution POP-related inventions
Source: Author's own elaboration

Table 1.2 Number of patent applications and growth rate by POP technology

	1991–2000		2001–2010	
Compound name	Number of patent applications	Average annual growth rate	Number of patent applications	Average annual growth rate
Aldrin	0	–	233	62.66%
Chlordane	134	5.44%	706	8.39%
Dieldrin	110	10.04%	934	23.42%
Endrin	124	10.00%	948	12.72%
Heptachlor	186	4.08%	573	5.12%
Hexachlorobenzene	474	3.64%	1874	5.22%
Mirex	56	15.69%	272	25.65%
PCBs	1	−10.00%	28	40.25%
Toxaphene	0	–	0	–
DDT	78	8.04%	723	4.61%
Pentachlorobenzene	23	1.66%	7	−8.75%
PCDD/F	642	6.65%	1121	1.03%

Source: Author's own elaboration

Note: The total number of patent applications by POP is larger than the unique number of POP-related patent applications because some applications are assigned to more than one POP and therefore counted multiple times

Figure 1.2 emphasizes some differences in the number of the patent applications related to the most patented POPs-related technologies.[3] Hexachlorobenzene- and chlordane-related patent applications are the technologies with the larger number of patents over the two periods. After 2001, hexachlorobenzene and endrin show the highest number of patent applications indicating innovative efforts in these technologies.

Next, I examine the trend of POP-related DOCDB patent families relative to the trend of patent families in the 'Manufacture of Pesticides and Other Agrochemical Products' (hereinafter 'pesticides') industry (20.2 NACE class code) which corresponds to the A01N and A01P IPC Class codes in the EPO-PATSTAT (Van Looy et al. 2014).[4] Figure 1.3 shows the evolution of the ratio of POP-related patent family applications over that of the technological class of pesticides, where the increase after the Stockholm Convention, observed in Fig. 1.1, becomes more pronounced.

[3] For the sake of clarity, I decided to report in Fig. 1.2 the number of the patent application for those POP disclosed in at least 500 patent applications.

[4] It is to note that POP-related inventions are prevalent in the "Manufacture of Pesticides and Other Agrochemical Products," which justifies the choice of this industry as our benchmark in the analyses (i.e. the share of their industry of application based on NACE classification ranges from 44% to 69% in the case of 20.2 NACE class code).

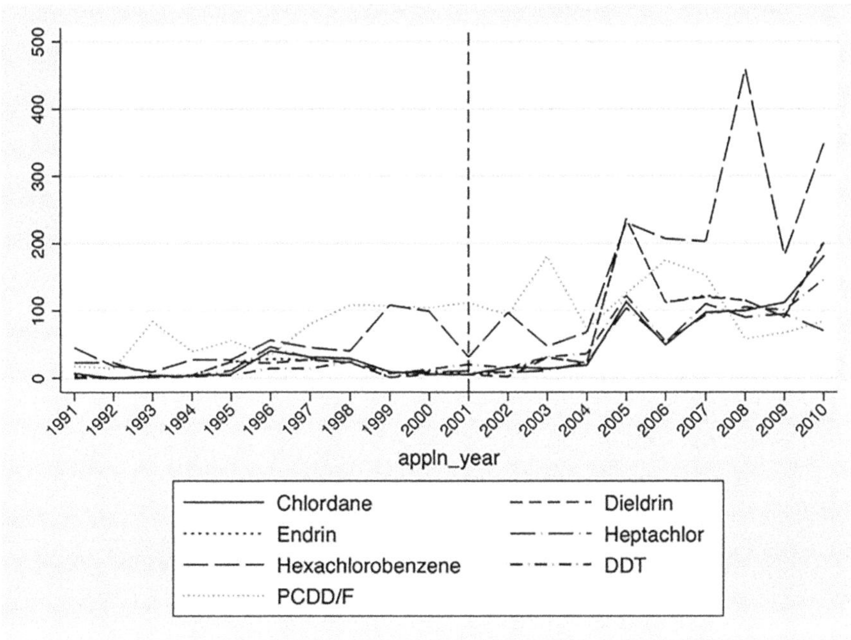

Fig. 1.2 Time evolution by POP technology
Source: Author's own elaboration
Note: The line plot shows the evolution in the number of patent application for those POP disclosed in at least 500 patent applications

1.3.2 Geographical Patterns

To protect an invention in multiple jurisdictions, the assignee needs to seek protection in different national patent offices and obtain different national patents. Figure 1.4 shows the geographic distribution of applications of patents belonging to the different POP-related patent applications, which are measured in terms of their percentile distribution (i.e. darker areas correspond to the top countries in terms of POP-related patent applications, while lighter areas correspond to bottom countries in the distribution of POP-related patent family applications) across two periods (i.e. 1991–2000 and 2001–2010). In the early stages of POP-related patent activities, the USA, Germany, and Japan stood out as the countries with higher innovative activities and as markets for such patents.

Patent applications to the EU and Japanese patent offices experienced a decline after the ban, while I observe a persistence at high levels in patent applications for the USA and an increase for China, Brazil, Argentina and Russia, despite having ratified the Stockholm Convention. To sum up, while the Stockholm Convention seems to have contributed to the increase of POP-related innovative activities both in relative and absolute terms, the geography shows also a geographical spread in several countries (in particular, emerging countries).

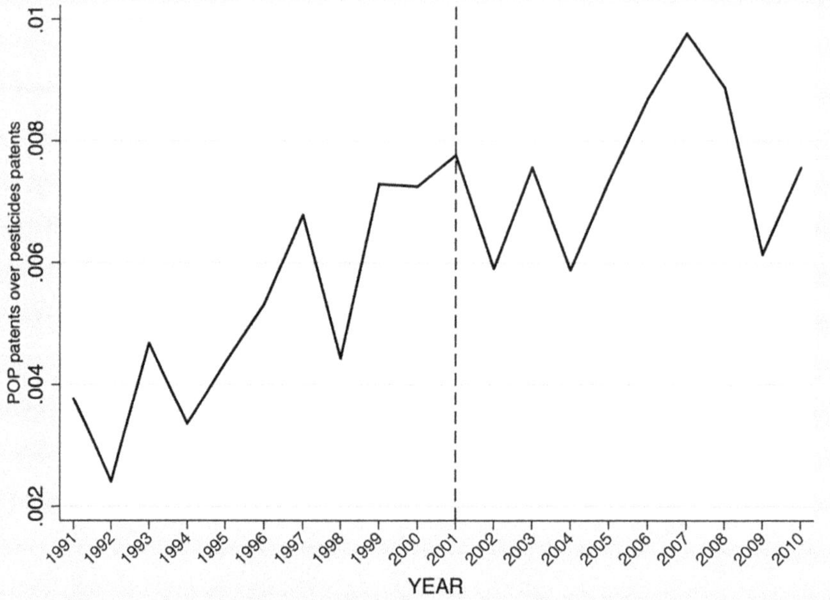

Fig. 1.3 Time evolution POP technologies/pesticide technologies
Source: Author's own elaboration

1.3.3 Organizational Patterns

Firms' innovative efforts may depend on the richness of technological opportunities as well as the strength of property rights (Levin et al. 1987). Following a long tradition in the literature, technological opportunities could be associated with low level of concentration of innovative activities, high entry rates as well as upheavals in the innovators' landscape (Breschi et al. 2000; Malerba and Orsenigo 1996; Martinelli et al. 2019). Moreover, in the chemical industry, entry into a new technology field is often assessed in light of opportunities to patent early, and understanding the drivers of patent strategy can shed light on subsequent R&D investments (Jayaraj and Gittelman 2018). Figure 1.5 depicts the evolution of the concentration of the innovative activities around each POP-related technology using the C4 indicator and the Herfindahl-Hirschman Index (HHI).

The C4 is the market share of the four largest firms in the industry. High values of C4 mean that the industry is strongly concentrated and controlled by only a few firms. Chlordane and hexachlorobenzene show high levels of C4 denoting a high concentration of innovative activities across the whole period of observation. Moreover, I used the HHI – calculated as the sum of squaring the market shares of the participating firms (Comanor and Scherer 1969) – to depict the dispersion of market concentration. Overall, the POP-related technologies display similar

(1991 – 2000)

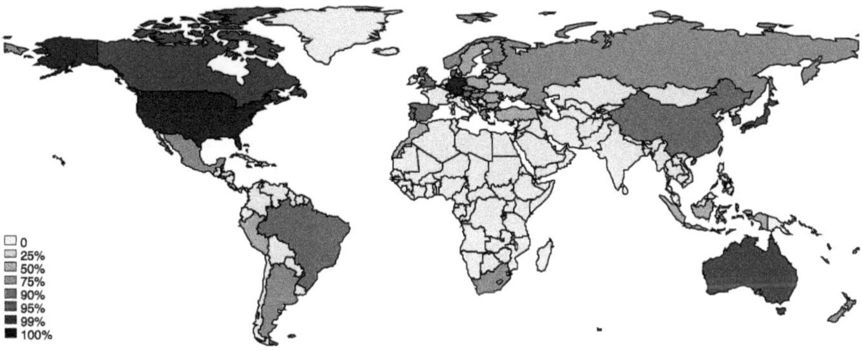

(a)

(2001 – 2010)

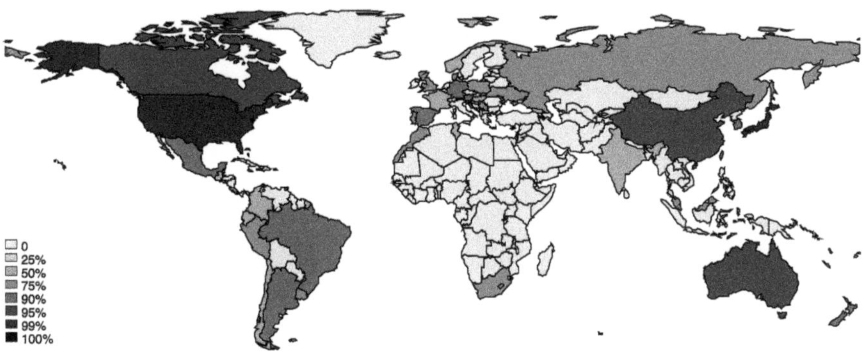

(b)

Fig. 1.4 Geographical distribution of POP technologies across countries
Source: Author's own elaboration

patterns, featuring a decrease in the share of top innovators and in market concentration. Considered together, results of C4 and HHI reflect the feature of the chemical industry in which, despite the crucial role played by large, diversified, multinational corporations and the high R&D intensity, market concentration is low (Gambardella et al. 2000).

Figure 1.6 shows the evolution of the Spearman correlation for the ranking of the top 10 patent applicants. The Spearman rank correlation indicates how the ranks of objects in one sample differ from the ranks in another sample. The values span from −1 to 1. A value of 1 indicates that the ranks are identical, while a value of −1 indicates that they are exactly inverted (Ginarte and Park 1997). Spearman correlation can therefore be used to capture the degree of technological turbulence across innovators. Overall, the POP-related technologies show a marked increase in the

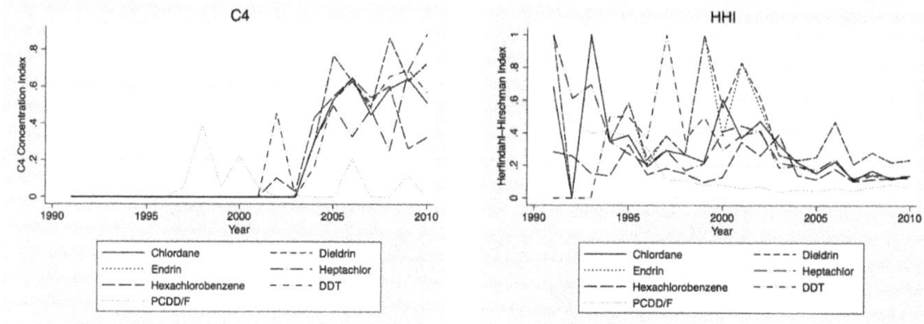

(a) (b)

Fig. 1.5 Evolution of the concentration of innovative activities by POP technology
Source: Author's own elaboration
Note: The line plot shows the evolution in the number of patent application for those POP disclosed in at least 500 patent applications

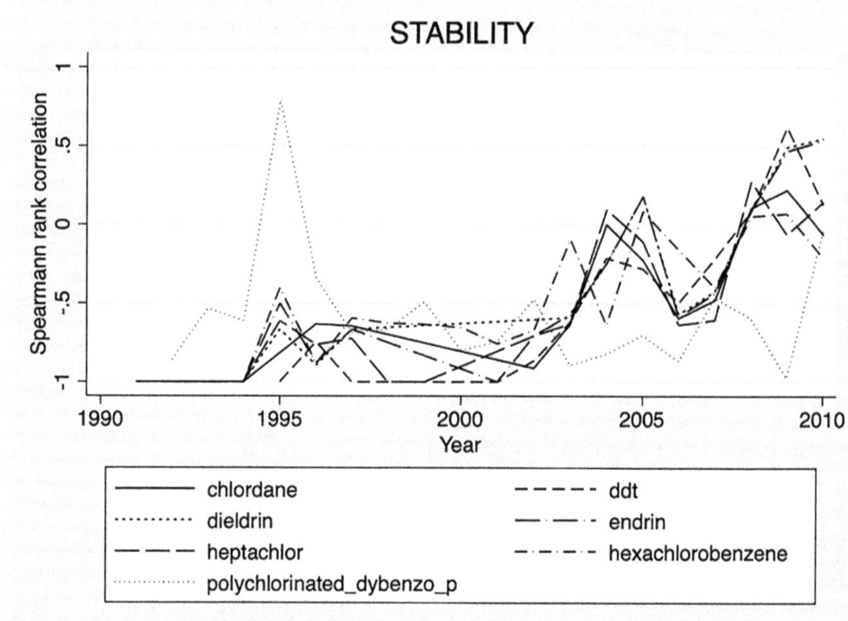

Fig. 1.6 Evolution of the stability of innovative activities across countries by POP technology
Source: Author's own elaboration
Note: The line plot shows the evolution in the number of patent application for those POP disclosed in at least 500 patent applications

stability over time, except for PCDD/F which shows very low levels of stability, denoting high mobility within the group of top applicants. The first decade (1991–2000) shows low level of stability among the 12 technologies under examination and increasing stability during the second decade (2001–2010). This result coupled with the following in Table 1.3 suggests a pattern of stability in technological leadership of the US, German and Swiss assignees of POP-related technologies.

Besides these general trends, it is interesting to zoom into each technology and identify the top patent assignee. Table 1.3 reports the list of the top 4 inventors for each POP-related technology for the period 1991–2000 and 2001–2010. It is interesting to note that the technological leadership during the first period under examination (1991–2000) belonged to Micro Flo Company, a US-based company which was the sole manufacturer of chlordane and heptachlor before the US ban (Lehr and Wiley 2004). Even considering deep changes in the production of pesticides and genetically modified seeds, environmental pressures and human health concerns, the technological leadership consolidates during the second period of observation toward the so-called Big 6 (i.e. Monsanto, Bayer, BASF, DuPont, Dow and Syngenta), which have recently experienced a process of mergers and acquisitions (M&A) (i.e. Dow-DuPont, Bayer-Monsanto and Syngenta-ChemChina). From a geographical point of view, I observe in Table 1.3 an increasing concentration of activities in the USA and Germany. Overall, technological leaders tend to overlap across the 12 technologies, especially during the second period of observation. Complementarities in use could explain the tendency of these companies to develop technological capabilities that strand across all the POP technologies.

Table 1.4 shows data on the industrial classification of POP-related technologies. To conduct such classification, I used the concordance table between IPC classes retrieved by the EPO PATSTAT database and 2-digit NACE (Rev. 2) codes developed by Van Looy et al. (2014). In addition to the NACE classes, the POP technologies have strong commonalities rooted in the manufacture of pesticides and other agrochemical products, manufacture of basic pharmaceutical products and pharmaceutical preparations and manufacture of basic chemicals.

1.4 Conclusions

Persistent organic pollutants are the first chemicals to be globally regulated by the 2001 Stockholm Convention. Attention to their noxious impact has only recently revamped because of their re-volatilization tied to climate change. However, while the environmental regulation was designed to forbid future production and use of these chemicals, it did not directly regulate the R&D processes underpinning the regulated technologies, perhaps based on the presumption that these would have been phased out too. Using a novel dataset of chemical patent applications, I find that environmental regulation as the Stockholm Convention had an impact on chemical industry. All the POP-related technologies show similar patterns of concentration and market dynamics. Overall, after the environmental regulation, I observe an increasing entry and industry growth and a decreasing of turbulence in the ranking of assignees. This results in an increasing number of new firms inventing around POP-related technologies as well as a consolidation of market share of leading patent assignees. The presence of large players (e.g. BASF, Bayer and Syngenta) in

Table 1.3 Top innovators over time by POP technology

Chemical	Leading innovators (1991–2000)	Country	Share	Leading innovators (2001–2010)	Country	Share
Chlordane	Micro Flo	US	20.00%	Bayer	DE	26.88%
	Agro-Chemie Noevenyvedoeszer	HU	10.00%	Syngenta	CH	15.25%
	Rohm & Haas	US	10.00%	Dow Chemical Company	US	5.63%
	Fiberchem	US	10.00%	Gat Microencapsulation	AT	5.00%
DDT	Micro Flo Corp	US	30.77%	Bayer	DE	27.39%
	Monsanto	US	15.38%	Syngenta	CH	17.20%
	Emil Flachsman	CH	15.38%	Dow Chemical Company	US	5.73%
	Dae Woong Pharma	KR	7.69%	Gat Microencapsulation	AT	5.10%
Dieldrin	Emil Flachsman	CH	31.58%	Du Pont	US	31.01%
	Micro Flo	US	21.05%	Syngenta	CH	18.39%
	Johnson & Johnson	US	21.05%	Dow Chemical Company	US	5.70%
	Amcol International	US	10.53%	Gat Microencapsulation	AT	5.06%
Endrin	Takara Bio	US	28.57%	Du Pont	US	29.88%
	Micro Flo	US	21.05%	Syngenta	CH	15.98%
	Emil Flachsman	CH	9.52%	Dow Chemical Company	US	5.49%
	Rohm & Haas	US	5%	Gat Microencapsulation	AT	4.88%
Heptachlor	Henkel	DE	28.95%	Bayer	DE	21.54%
	Micro Flo	US	10.53%	Syngenta	CH	8.27%
	Rhone Poulenc Chimie	FR	10.53%	Dow Chemical Company	US	6.02%
	Glaxo Smith Kline	GB	5.26%	Foamix	US	3.76%
Hexachlorobenzene	Idea	DE	16.22%	Syngenta	CH	14.44%
	Foamix	US	6.31%	BASF	DE	30.77%
	3M	US	6.31%	Bayer	DE	7.94%
	Idemitsu Petrochemical	JP	1.80%	Walter Harald	DE	4.47%

PCDD/F	Ebara Corp	JP	9.55%	BASF	DE	4.24%
	Orient Green Co	ID	7.30%	Bayer	US	4.24%
	Glaxo Smith Kline	GB	5.62%	Dow Chemical Company	US	3.89%
	Maruto Kk	JP	5.06%	Syngenta	CH	3.89%

Source: Author's own elaboration

Table 1.4 Industrial sectors by POP technology

Chemical	NACE Rev. 2 class	Share	NACE Rev. 2 class	Share
Chlordane	Manufacture of basic chemicals, fertilizers and nitrogen compounds, plastics and synthetic rubber in primary forms	32.31%	Manufacture of pesticides and other agrochemical products	55.70%
	Manufacture of pesticides and other agrochemical products	26.53%	Manufacture of basic pharmaceutical products and pharmaceutical preparations	27.59%
	Manufacture of basic pharmaceutical products and pharmaceutical preparations	14.29%	Manufacture of basic chemicals, fertilizers and nitrogen compounds, plastics and synthetic rubber in primary forms	3.54%
	Manufacture of other chemical products	9.86%	Manufacture of agricultural and forestry machinery	2.48%
DDT	Manufacture of basic pharmaceutical products and pharmaceutical preparations	23.39%	Manufacture of pesticides and other agrochemical products	44.14%
	Manufacture of pesticides and other agrochemical products	21.64%	Manufacture of basic pharmaceutical products and pharmaceutical preparations	28.74%
	Manufacture of basic chemicals, fertilizers, and nitrogen compounds, plastics and synthetic rubber in primary forms	21.05%	Manufacture of basic chemicals, fertilizers and nitrogen compounds, plastics and synthetic rubber in primary forms	3.39%
	Manufacture of other chemical products	10.53%	Manufacture of food products	3.08%
Dieldrin	Manufacture of pesticides and other agrochemical products	25.91%	Manufacture of pesticides and other agrochemical products	45.12%
	Manufacture of basic chemicals, fertilizers and nitrogen compounds, plastics and synthetic rubber in primary forms	24.55%	Manufacture of basic pharmaceutical products and pharmaceutical preparations	34.00%
	Manufacture of basic pharmaceutical products and pharmaceutical preparations	13.18%	Manufacture of basic chemicals, fertilizers and nitrogen compounds, plastics and synthetic rubber in primary forms	2.57%
	Manufacture of other chemical products	12.27%	Manufacture of food products	2.28%

(continued)

Table 1.4 (continued)

Chemical	NACE Rev. 2 class	Share	NACE Rev. 2 class	Share
Endrin	Manufacture of basic chemicals, fertilizers and nitrogen compounds, plastics and synthetic rubber in primary forms	24.79%	Manufacture of pesticides and other agrochemical products	44.26%
	Manufacture of pesticides and other agrochemical products	23.55%	Manufacture of basic pharmaceutical products and pharmaceutical preparations	33.63%
	Manufacture of basic pharmaceutical products and pharmaceutical preparations	12.81%	Manufacture of other chemical products	2.57%
	Manufacture of other chemical products	11.16%	Manufacture of basic chemicals, fertilizers and nitrogen compounds, plastics and synthetic rubber in primary forms	2.52%
Heptachlor	Manufacture of basic chemicals, fertilizers, and nitrogen compounds, plastics and synthetic rubber in primary forms	28.97%	Manufacture of pesticides and other agrochemical products	48.73%
	Manufacture of pesticides and other agrochemical products	25.38%	Manufacture of basic pharmaceutical products and pharmaceutical preparations	27.42%
	Manufacture of basic pharmaceutical products and pharmaceutical preparations	15.90%	Manufacture of basic chemicals, fertilizers and nitrogen compounds, plastics and synthetic rubber in primary forms	5.88%
	Manufacture of other chemical products	10.00%	Manufacture of food products	2.19%

(continued)

Table 1.4 (continued)

Chemical	NACE Rev. 2 class	Share	NACE Rev. 2 class	Share
Hexachlorobenzene	Manufacture of basic pharmaceutical products and pharmaceutical preparations	21.69%	Manufacture of pesticides and other agrochemical products	48.25%
	Manufacture of medical and dental instruments and supplies	11.97%	Manufacture of basic pharmaceutical products and pharmaceutical preparations	15.34%
	Manufacture of basic chemicals, fertilizers and nitrogen compounds, plastics and synthetic rubber in primary forms	10.79%	Manufacture of soap and detergents, cleaning and polishing preparations, perfumes and toilet preparations	5.53%
	Manufacture of soap and detergents, cleaning and polishing preparations, perfumes and toilet preparations	8.93%	Manufacture of basic chemicals, fertilizers and nitrogen compounds, plastics and synthetic rubber in primary forms	5.31%
PCDD/F	Manufacture of basic pharmaceutical products and pharmaceutical preparations	30.24%	Manufacture of basic pharmaceutical products and pharmaceutical preparations	31.13%
	Manufacture of basic chemicals, fertilizers and nitrogen compounds, plastics and synthetic rubber in primary forms	17.50%	Manufacture of basic chemicals, fertilizers and nitrogen compounds, plastics and synthetic rubber in primary forms	17.02%
	Manufacture of instruments and appliances for measuring, testing and navigation; watches and clocks	13.06%	Manufacture of other chemical products	7.99%
	Manufacture of other general-purpose machinery	7.58%	Manufacture of instruments and appliances for measuring, testing and navigation; watches and clocks	7.43%

Source: Author's own elaboration

POP-related technologies could, however, limit entry by small innovative firms and provide scope for agglomeration and diversification strategies. This study reveals that there has been a global increase in POP-related patent applications after 2001 which resulted also in an increase in a range of new countries, other than the USA, EU and Japan where POP-related inventions were first filed in history. Emerging economies like Russia, China and Brazil as well as other countries (Argentina) where the agro-food industry is a driver of economic growth witnessed an increase in the number of POP-related patent applications after the Stockholm Convention ratification year (2004). Yet, given the high volatility of POPs, such increases are a matter of concerns also for countries where POP-related applications have been steadily diminishing. I am not surprised to see that companies seek intellectual property protection in emerging markets, as this is very much consistent with the pollution haven hypothesis and can fit into a story where these companies seek to extend the life cycle of the old (banned) technologies as long as possible. Along these lines, the Stockholm Convention was a technological disruption that impacted the chemical industry which allows the entry of new firms in chemical market.

References

Bekkers, Rudi, Arianna Martinelli, and Federico Tamagni. 2020. The impact of including standards-related documentation in patent prior art: Evidence from an EPO policy change. *Research Policy* 49 (7): 104007. https://doi.org/10.1016/j.respol.2020.104007.
Biggi, Gianluca, and Elisa Giuliani. 2020. The noxious consequences of innovation: What do we know? *Industry and Innovation*: 1–23. https://doi.org/10.1080/13662716.2020.1726729.
Breschi, Stefano, Franco Malerba, and Luigi Orsenigo. 2000. Technological regimes and Schumpeterian patterns of innovation. *The Economic Journal* 110 (463): 388–410. https://doi.org/10.1111/1468-0297.00530.
Comanor, William S., and Frederic M. Scherer. 1969. Patent statistics as a measure of technical change. *Journal of Political Economy* 77 (3): 392–398.
Gambardella, A., L. Orsenigo, and Fabio Pammolli. 2000. *Global competitiveness in pharmaceuticals: A European perspective*. Brussels: European Commission.
Ginarte, J.C., and W. Park. 1997. Determinants of patent rights: A cross-national study. *Research Policy* 26 (3): 283–301.
Griliches, Zvi. 1990. Patent statistics as economic indicators: A survey. *Journal of Economic Literature* 28 (4): 1661–1707.
Hall, B.H., and D. Haroff. 2012. Recent research on the economics of patents. In NBER working paper No. w17773.
Hall, J.K., and M.J.C. Martin. 2005. Disruptive technologies, stakeholders and the innovation value-added chain: A framework for evaluating radical technology development. *R & D Management* 35 (3): 273–284. https://doi.org/10.1111/j.1467-9310.2005.00389.x.
Hall, Bronwyn H., Adam B. Jaffe, and Manuel Trajtenberg. 2001. *The NBER patent citation data file: Lessons, insights and methodological tools*. Cambridge: NBER.
Harhoff, Dietmar, Francis Narin, Frederic M. Scherer, and Katrin Vopel. 1999. Citation frequency and the value of patented inventions. *Review of Economics and Statistics* 81 (3): 511–515.
Harhoff, Dietmar, Frederic M. Scherer, and Katrin Vopel. 2003. Citations, family size, opposition and the value of patent rights. *Research Policy* 32 (8): 1343–1363.
Jaffe, Adam B., and Gaétan de Rassenfosse. 2017. Patent citation data in social science research: Overview and best practices. *Journal of the Association for Information Science and Technology* 68 (6): 1360–1374. https://doi.org/10.1002/asi.23731.
Jayaraj, Sebastian, and Michelle Gittelman. 2018. Impact of scientific maps on technological search and novelty. *Academy of Management Proceedings* 2018 (1): 15414. https://doi.org/10.5465/ambpp.2018.234.
Kuhn, Jeffrey M., and N. Thompson. 2017. The ways we've been measuring patent scope are wrong: How to measure and draw causal inferences with patent scope. Available at SSRN 2977273.
Kuhn, Jeffrey M., and Neil C. Thompson. 2019. How to measure and draw causal inferences with patent scope. *International Journal of the Economics of Business* 26 (1): 5–38.

Lanjouw, Jean O., and Mark Schankerman. 2001. Characteristics of patent litigation: A window on competition. *RAND Journal of Economics* 32: 129–151.

Lanjouw, Jean O., Ariel Pakes, and Jonathan Putnam. 1998. How to count patents and value intellectual property: The uses of patent renewal and application data. *The Journal of Industrial Economics* 46 (4): 405–432.

Lehr, Jay H., and John Wiley. 2004. *Wiley's remediation technologies handbook: Major contaminant chemicals and chemical groups*. New York: Wiley.

Lerner, Joshua. 1994. The importance of patent scope: An empirical analysis. *The Rand Journal of Economics* 25: 319–333.

Levin, Richard, Alvin Klevorick, Richard Nelson, and Sidney Winter. 1987. Appropriating the Returns from Industrial R&D. *Brookings Papers on Economic Activity* 18: 783–832. https://doi.org/10.2307/2534454.

Malerba, Franco, and Luigi Orsenigo. 1996. Schumpeterian patterns of innovation are technology-specific. *Research Policy* 25 (3): 451–478.

Marco, Alan C., Joshua D. Sarnoff, and Charles A.W. deGrazia. 2019. Patent claims and patent scope. *Research Policy* 48 (9): 103790. https://doi.org/10.1016/j.respol.2019.04.014.

Martinelli, Arianna, Andrea Mina, and Massimo Moggi. 2019. *The enabling technologies of industry 4.0: Examining the seeds of the fourth industrial revolution*. LEM Working Paper Series.

Martínez, C. 2011. Patent families: When do different definitions really matter? *Scientometrics* 86 (1): 39–63. https://doi.org/10.1007/s11192-010-0251-3.

Meadows, Donella, Jorgen Randers, and Dennis Meadows. 2004. *Limits to growth: The 30-year update*. Chelsea: Green Publishing.

Papadatos, George, Mark Davies, Nathan Dedman, Jon Chambers, Anna Gaulton, James Siddle, Richard Koks, Sean A. Irvine, Joe Pettersson, and Nicko Goncharoff. 2016. SureChEMBL: A large-scale, chemically annotated patent document database. *Nucleic Acids Research* 44 (D1): D1220–D1228.

Schankerman, Mark, and Ariel Pakes. 1985. *Estimates of the value of patent rights in European countries during the Post-1950 period*. Cambridge: National Bureau of Economic Research.

Schot, Johan, and W. Edward Steinmueller. 2018. Three frames for innovation policy: R&D, systems of innovation and transformative change. *Research Policy* 47 (9): 1554–1567.

Steffen, Will, Reinhold Leinfelder, Jan Zalasiewicz, Colin N. Waters, Mark Williams, Colin Summerhayes, Anthony D. Barnosky, Alejandro Cearreta, Paul Crutzen, Matt Edgeworth, Erle C. Ellis, Ian J. Fairchild, Agnieszka Galuszka, Jacques Grinevald, Alan Haywood, Juliana Ivar do Sul, Catherine Jeandel, J.R. McNeill, Eric Odada, Naomi Oreskes, Andrew Revkin, Daniel deB Richter, James Syvitski, Davor Vidas, Michael Wagreich, Scott L. Wing, Alexander P. Wolfe, and H.J. Schellnhuber. 2016. Stratigraphic and earth system approaches to defining the anthropocene. *Earth's Future* 4 (8): 324–345. https://doi.org/10.1002/2016EF000379.

Trajtenberg, Manuel. 1990. A penny for your quotes: Patent citations and the value of innovations. *The Rand Journal of Economics* 21: 172–187.

Van Looy, Bart, Caro Vereyen, and Ulrich Schmoch. 2014. *Patent statistics: Concordance IPC V8–NACE rev. 2*. Luxembourg: Eurostat, European Commission.

Chapter 2
Assessing Policy Impact on Chemical Inventions: The Case of the Stockholm Convention

Abstract Once companies develop hazardous products which can be dangerous for the environment and human health, it takes very long for regulatory bodies to ban these products. However, very little is known about the impact of regulatory action on firms' inventive strategies. Using a difference-in-difference approach, I test the impact of regulation on a sample of POP-related patents against a control sample of untreated pesticides. Interestingly, I find that the signature and/or ratification of Stockholm Convention – the UN ban on the use, trade and production of persistent organic pollutants – increases the rate of POP-related invention and new compound patenting, opening up interesting questions about corporate innovative strategies and calling for further research on the nature of the new POP-related inventions.

2.1 Introduction

There is a lot to worry about climate change, but bioscientists have one specific concern: the revolatilization of persistent organic pollutants (POPs) following the melting of polar ice (Nizzetto et al. 2010; Ma et al. 2011; Rigét et al. 2019). POPs are defined as 'chemical substances that persist in the environment, bio-accumulate through the food chain, and pose a risk of causing adverse effects to human health and the environment' (Fitzgerald and Wikoff 2014). The reason why there is so much concern about their revolatilization in the atmosphere is that they are highly hazardous: they cause cancer, damage the immune and nervous systems and are highly poisonous for human beings, animal species and the environment at large (Kodavanti et al. 2014). For this reason, following the recommendation of the Intergovernmental Forum on Chemical Safety (IFCS) and the International Programme on Chemical Safety (IPCS), a first group of a hazardous POPs, also known as the 'Dirty Dozen' (namely, dieldrin, aldrin, chlordane, DDT, endrin, heptachlor, hexachlorobenzene, mirex, pentachlorobenzene, toxaphene, polychlorinated biphenyls (PCBs), and polychlorinated dibenzo-p-dioxins (PCDD/F)), were banned, or their use was severely restricted starting from 2001 by an international

G. Biggi, *Industrial Dynamics and Firm Strategies in the Agrochemical Industry*, SpringerBriefs in Economics, https://doi.org/10.1007/978-3-031-52689-3_2

treaty – the Stockholm Convention. The treaty was signed between 2001 and 2002 by 153 countries worldwide, and it was progressively ratified in the following years (most ratifications occurred between 2001 and 2007). This global ban has mitigated concerns about these hazardous chemicals at least up until very recently when it became clear that they would re-volatilize in the atmosphere as a consequence of melting Antarctic ice.

Yet, while most research has addressed the legacy of POPs, very little is known about their future. Are these chemicals and their knowledge really disappearing? Are companies and other inventing organizations conducting research and development (R&D) programs around those compounds? More specifically, beside banning use and production, has the Stockholm Convention also impacted on the way firms patent POP-related inventions through time and across geographies? Despite the fact that a handful of countries has not yet ratified the treaty (e.g. the USA, Israel, Malaysia and Italy), I consider the Stockholm Convention as a global treaty. This is because even in the case of lack of ratification, countries have often taken steps to regulate POP production and use within their jurisdictions even prior to the Stockholm Convention. For instance, the USA has implemented several measures that mirror the treaty's regulations such as the agreement with Canada for the Virtual Elimination of Persistent Toxic Substances in the Great Lakes and the North American Agreement on Environmental Cooperation (NAAEC), which developed a regional initiative on the management of chemicals, including persistent organic pollutant. I consider the universe of POP-related patent applications from 1991 to 2010 amounting to 5250 patent applications grouped in 624 DOCDB patent families. I then examine their disclosed groups of compounds to unpack temporal to unpack the role of environmental regulation on the rate of invention and compound production by chemical firms included in my sample.

2.2 Theory

2.2.1 Global Environmental Challenges and Their Regulation

The exposure of people and their ecosystems to environmental hazards is a classical 'tragedy of the commons' (Hardin 1968; Ansari et al. 2013), and when these hazards have no borders but spread quickly across geographical space to become planetary problems, global regulation and governance are invoked as a necessary step to fix the problem. Global regulations and treaties may be successful or not. According to recent statistics, the 1987 Montreal Protocol has allowed for the dramatic decline in global ozone-depleting emissions, while the Kyoto Protocol (and subsequent related protocols) to reduce carbon dioxide (CO_2) emissions and the presence of greenhouse gases (GHG) in the atmosphere have, to the date of writing, been unable to meet their targets. The reasons why countries and their organizations may fail to meet vital environmental goals are complex and manifold, but often governments are blamed for failing to seriously impose environmental regulations in their territories or jurisdictions, often despite having ratified or signed the relevant treaties

(Bates 2008; Scherer and Palazzo 2011; Hart and Zingales 2017). Against this background, economists show that when national environmental regulations are strictly enforced, environmental pollution decreases (Shapiro and Walker 2018). Hence, when treaties are binding and regulations are strictly enforced by the national states, compliance on the side of companies is to be expected because the sanctions inherent in noncompliance are likely to be severe and discourage deviance from the norm. Bans may produce their effects in a short time (e.g. in the case of the Montreal Protocol, the production of new stocks of chlorofluorocarbon (CFC) ceased in virtually all countries at around the same time) or take longer, but the expectation is that eventually they will lead to the discontinuation of the banned technology in its production and use.

2.2.2 *Responses to Banned Technologies: Hypotheses*

In evolutionary perspectives, innovations have two dimensions: technical novelty and market selection, and firm innovative activities are aimed at developing novelty of economic value (Nelson 2009). The generation of technical novelty – driven by new knowledge and technology – leads to diversity and a better chance of market selection. In this search for technical novelty, firms can both explore new technological space and exploit prior knowledge (March 1991). The balance depends on the relative costs of exploration and exploitation and the ability to apply prior expertise towards future innovations. Exploration is costly and risky, and the balance with exploitation depends on their relative cost. The idea of induced innovation (Hicks 1963) recognizes that R&D is a profit-motivated activity and that the direction of innovation likely corresponds positively to the direction of increased relative cost. Environmental regulation can spur exploration reducing its relative cost. Scholars indicate that environmental regulation can spur firms' ability to innovate, by lowering the relative cost of exploration. That regulation can help direct towards more useful new product, processes or technologies (Fleming and Sorenson 2004). Thus, environmental regulation is theorized as allowing firms to enlarge their innovative outcomes. New knowledge occurs when new information is integrated and/or recombined with existing knowledge of the problem giving rise to breakthrough ideas and innovations (Schilling and Green 2011). In the chemical sector, environmental regulation can trigger the transformation process of existing chemical compounds and substances. In that context, my hypotheses suggest that, after a ban, companies and other inventing entities will take new 'explorative' innovation paths (March 1991) and therefore will make new knowledge around the regulated technologies. They will also potentially explore radically new technological trajectories (Dosi 1982), which I envisage will not build on the established technological knowledge. The general rationale for this is that the banned technological knowledge becomes a dangerous terrain for new investments, especially if the new technological developments draw – even if partially – on the banned technological knowledge that can be subject to future bans within the same or a different treaty. Hence, in a scenario of heightened uncertainty and risk following a global ban, I expect the following hypothesis to be supported:

Hypothesis 1 (a): Environmental regulation will increase overall inventive activity around regulated technologies.

Hypothesis 1 (b): Environmental regulation will alter technological inventive strategies around regulated technologies.

Both hypotheses assume that companies and other organizations conducting research around the regulated technologies are not malevolent entities and will therefore have agreed on the threats posed by their past discoveries and will seek to find ways to address them in the future, in order to stop or minimize the noxious impacts on humans and the environment. The direction of their R&D efforts after the ban is also assumed to be the result of calculated strategic decisions in the face of a changing regulatory environment; such decisions are expected to be taken in order to both address social and environmental threats and to hedge against future losses in the case of more stringent regulatory measures.

2.3 Methods

2.3.1 Data

In this study, I am interested in testing the impact of the Stockholm Convention on chemical patenting. To measure the effects of the environmental regulation, I look for external indicators of early-stage R&D activity that could be both comprehensive across the industry and also accurate. In innovation and strategic management research, patent data are widely used and adopted measures of innovation and have been traditionally used to proxy R&D activities and knowledge creation of firms, research institutes and universities (Jaffe 1986; Jaffe et al. 1993). Along these lines, I collect a novel dataset of chemical patents to test the technological search and innovation before and after the Stockholm Convention. The following section provides an introduction to chemical patenting by providing a more fine-grained description of the data collection process pursued in this study.

2.3.2 Chemical Patenting

To protect their chemical inventions, firms or other entities patent their newly invented compound or a new combination of compounds by way of Markush structure. Markush structures are characterized by a special placeholder structure called Markush structure to capture a set of compounds. Figure 2.1 shows a Markush structure claiming a range of compounds.

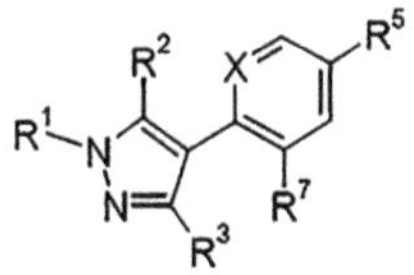

(I)

wherein

R^1 is C_1-C_4alkyl or C_1-C_4haloalkyl;

R^2 is an optionally substituted aryl or heteroaryl;

R^3 is halogen;

R^4 is hydrogen, halogen, C_1-C_4 alkyl, C_1-C_4 haloalkyl, cyano or OR^6;

R^5 is hydrogen, halogen, C_1-C_4 alkyl, C_1-C_4 haloalkyl, cyano or OR^6;

R^6 is hydrogen, C_1-C_6 alkyl, C_3-C_7 cycloalkyl, C_3-C_{10} alkylcycloalkyl, C_1-C_6 haloalkyl, C_2-C_6 alkenyl, C_2-C_6 haloalkenyl, C_3-C_7 cycloalkenyl, C_2-C_6 alkynyl, C_2-C_6 haloalkynyl, C_2-C_6 alkyloxyalkyl;

R^7 is halogen or OR^6;

X is N or C-R^4;

or an agrochemically usable salt form thereof.

Fig. 2.1 Example of Markush structure
Source: Drawn from Markush Editor (ChemAxon)

In Fig. 2.1, R1–R7 are placeholders that can accept different chemical compounds for each position. In this case, R1 has two options while R3 has only one option. Instead of listing all the possible combinations, the Markush structure captures this combinatorial set of compounds. A Markush structure is used in patent applications to define the scope of the chemical protection sought in a patent document. Markush patents can try to capture a broad spectrum of compounds sometimes resulting into thousands of combinations.[1] Markush patents are filed very early in the discovery stage where a firm makes general claims for a number of compounds without revealing the identity of the exact compound or compounds it is pursuing. In chemical industry, Markush patents are considered the starting point where firms begin to claim intellectual property rights by planting 'flags' in chemical space (Southall and Ajay 2006). The compounds of interest are hidden among hundreds of other similar-looking compounds with the same basic structures. An interesting feature of Markush patents is that they encapsulate the actual compounds made and those that the firm or inventor plans to protect for future use – sometimes, running into the hundreds of newly invented compounds. Thus, these compounds within Markush patents represent the explorative effort undertaken by the firm or inventor in chemical field. These unique properties of Markush structures in patents make them extremely useful for analysing the evolution of technological search and innovation by firms. In this study, I exploit these unique features of Markush structures in patents to measure R&D activity and track search trajectories over time.

[1] It is to note that if the structure of Markush claims is too broad, the patent can be rejected by the patent examiner.

2.3.3 Data Collection

I rely on two main databases: the chemical database of the European Molecular Biology Laboratory SureChEMBL and the EPO-PATSTAT. SureChEMBL is a publicly available large-scale database (Papadatos et al. 2016) which has the unique feature of providing comprehensive compound-patent association maps and related Markush structures in patent claims. The SureChEMBL database provides also information on chemical compound international identifiers (i.e. SureChEMBL identifier, SMILES or standard InChIKey) that allow to precisely search all the patents related to a specific compound. To retrieve all the patents associated with each POP, I use one or multiple CAS Registry Number identifiers related to POPs. Most importantly, the SureChEMBL database allows us to identify all patents that cite a POP in its claims, which are the extent (i.e. the scope) of the protection sought in a patent application (Kuhn and Thompson 2019; Bekkers et al. 2020; Jayaraj and Gittelman 2018; Marco et al. 2019) described by way of Markush structures.

For the study, I am interested in capturing effects of the Stockholm Convention on chemical patenting and needed a sample set that included pre- and post-patents of POPs (between 2001 and 2004). Though the Stockholm Convention was signed in 2001, its ratification by most of the signatory countries was not completed until 2004. I restricted the search for patent applications filed between 1991 and 2010 to cover a window of time broad enough to measure pre- and post-effects of the Convention. This resulted in a dataset of 5240 patent records, comprised of 1026 granted patents and 4214 patent applications.

2.3.4 Sample Selection

The search in SureChEMBL identifies 1113 POP-related patent applications at European Patent Office (EPO), US Patent Office (USPTO), Japan Patent Office (JPO), and World Intellectual Property Organization (WIPO) between 1991 and 2010. I decided to focus on patent applications because they give a window onto the exploratory efforts of assignees, unlike granted patent, which only represent a small percentage of the filed applications. Some of the retrieved patent applications might protect the same invention in multiple legislations among the four available in the ChEMBL database. To avoid double or multiple count, I focus our analysis at the unique DOCDB patent family level. I then use the EPO-PATSTAT (version Autumn 2018) database to identify the DOCDB patent families for all the POP-related patent applications retrieved from the ChEMBL database. The final set includes 624 unique DOCDB patent families including 5240 patent applications filed in 75 patent authorities of which 233 (2.52%) were related to aldrin, 840 (9.08%) related to chlordane, 1044 (11.29%) related to dieldrin, 1072 (11.59%) related to endrin, 759 (8.21%) related to heptachlor, 2348 (25.39%) related to hexachlorobenzene, 328 (3.55%) related to mirex, 29 (0.31%) related to polychlorinated biphenyls (PCBs), 801 (8.66%) related to DDT, 30 (0.32%) related to pentachlorobenzene, and 624 (19.07%) related to polychlorinated dibenzo-p-dioxins.

Assignees were extracted from patent records and stored separately. Assignees have a name and location associated with them. Each assignee is categorized into a separate category: firms, individual inventors and universities. This classification process yielded 5994 firms, 1382 individual inventors and 327 universities.[2] For the analysis, only firms were selected and the analysis does not include any collaborations between firms or between academia and industry.

2.3.5 *Identification Strategy*

Throughout interviews to chemistry researcher and patent examiners, I tried to understand how to identify firm's patenting strategies in relation to a specific chemical compound. Chemical patents within their Markus structures would normally disclose the compound chemical structure with specific keywords that indicated the search strategy used to make the compounds. To identify the presence of POP-related compounds, SureChEMBL provides a human curated field (see Fig. 2.2) which translates the compound name disclosed in the Markush structure into international chemical identities of the compound structures as the CAS Registry Numbers, or SMILES or InChIKey. Using this combined data, the patent claim section from the SureChEMBL was scanned and downloaded for this purpose.

2.4 Research Design

2.4.1 *Dependent Variables*

Number of Compounds in Patent Claims Each compound listed in patent claims is a chemical entity with a unique chemical structure. These chemical compounds compose the invention sought in the patent document and substantiate patent claims. Hence, a set of compounds in a patent indicate the firm's search activity in within the chemical field and the intent to protect a portion of the 'chemical space'. The number of compounds encoded in chemical patents is then a factor of explorative search effort, dedicated resources and strategic intent of the firm and inventors (Drews 2000; DiMasi et al. 2010). A lot of compounds in patent claims imply large search efforts and knowledge flows within the firm (Jaffe and Trajtenberg 1999; Henderson and Cockburn 1996). Thus, a number of patented compounds provide a quantitative representation of the intensity of search effort and can be proxied as a measure of chemical innovation.

[2] It is to note that the cumulative number of assignees (including firms, individual inventors and universities) is higher than the total number of the patent application in the dataset. This can be ascribed to the fact that a single patent application can be filed by multiple firms (e.g. collaborative R&D) or individual inventors.

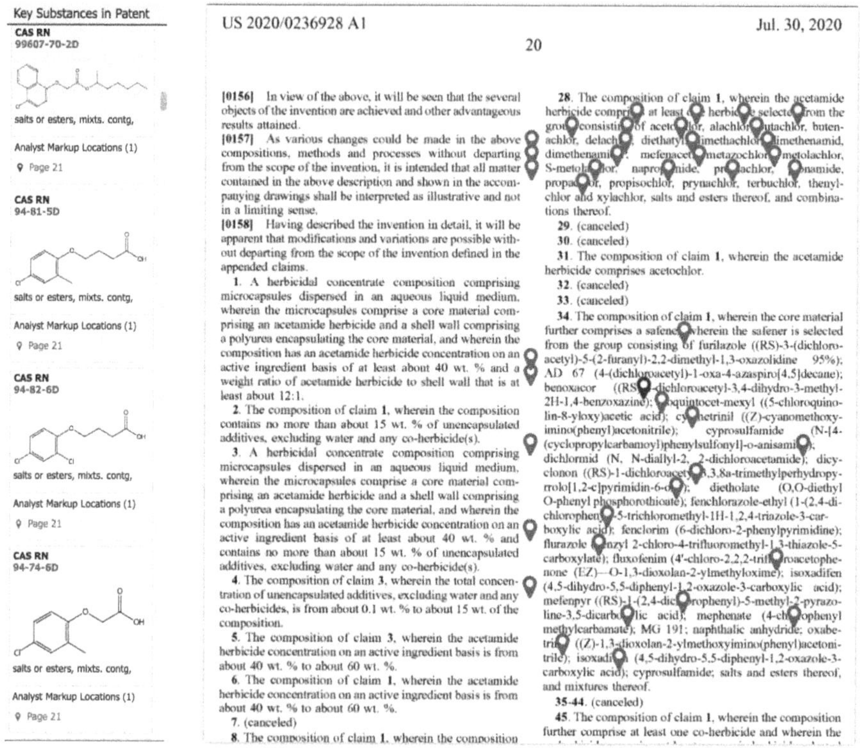

Key Substances in Patent

CAS RN 99607-70-2D — salts or esters, mixts. contg, — Analyst Markup Locations (1) — Page 21

CAS RN 94-81-5D — salts or esters, mixts. contg, — Analyst Markup Locations (1) — Page 21

CAS RN 94-82-6D — salts or esters, mixts. contg, — Analyst Markup Locations (1) — Page 21

CAS RN 94-74-6D — salts or esters, mixts. contg, — Analyst Markup Locations (1) — Page 21

US 2020/0236928 A1 — 20 — Jul. 30, 2020

[0156] In view of the above, it will be seen that the several objects of the invention are achieved and other advantageous results attained.

[0157] As various changes could be made in the above compositions, methods and processes without departing from the scope of the invention, it is intended that all matter contained in the above description and shown in the accompanying drawings shall be interpreted as illustrative and not in a limiting sense.

[0158] Having described the invention in detail, it will be apparent that modifications and variations are possible without departing from the scope of the invention defined in the appended claims.

1. A herbicidal concentrate composition comprising microcapsules dispersed in an aqueous liquid medium, wherein the microcapsules comprise a core material comprising an acetamide herbicide and a shell wall comprising a polyurea encapsulating the core material, and wherein the composition has an acetamide herbicide concentration on an active ingredient basis of at least about 40 wt. % and a weight ratio of acetamide herbicide to shell wall that is at least about 12:1.

2. The composition of claim 1, wherein the composition contains no more than about 15 wt. % of unencapsulated additives, excluding water and any co-herbicide(s).

3. A herbicidal concentrate composition comprising microcapsules dispersed in an aqueous liquid medium, wherein the microcapsules comprise a core material comprising an acetamide herbicide and a shell wall comprising a polyurea encapsulating the core material, and wherein the composition has an acetamide herbicide concentration on an active ingredient basis of at least about 40 wt. % and contains no more than about 15 wt. % of unencapsulated additives, excluding water and any co-herbicide(s).

4. The composition of claim 3, wherein the total concentration of unencapsulated additives, excluding water and any co-herbicides, is from about 0.1 wt. % to about 15 wt. of the composition.

5. The composition of claim 3, wherein the acetamide herbicide concentration on an active ingredient basis is from about 40 wt. % to about 60 wt. %.

6. The composition of claim 1, wherein the acetamide herbicide concentration on an active ingredient basis is from about 40 wt. % to about 60 wt. %.

7. (canceled)

8. The composition of claim 1, wherein the composition

28. The composition of claim 1, wherein the acetamide herbicide compri[…] at least […] herbic[…] selecte[…] from the gro[…] consisti[…] of acet[…]lor, alachlor, […]tachlor, butenachlor, delach[…], diethatyl, […]imethachlor, […]imethenamid, dimethenami[…], mefenacet, metazochlor, metolachlor, S-metol[…]lor, napro[…]mide, pr[…]achlor, […]namide, propa[…]or, propisochlor, prynachlor, terbuchlor, thenylchlor and xylachlor, salts and esters thereof, and combinations thereof.

29. (canceled)

30. (canceled)

31. The composition of claim 1, wherein the acetamide herbicide comprises acetochlor.

32. (canceled)

33. (canceled)

34. The composition of claim 1, wherein the core material further comprises a safene[…] wherein the safener is selected from the group consisting of furilazole ((RS)-3-(dichloroacetyl)-5-(2-furanyl)-2,2-dimethyl-1,3-oxazolidine 95%); AD 67 (4-(dichloroacetyl)-1-oxa-4-azaspiro[4.5]decane); benoxacor ((RS[…]-dichloroacetyl-3,4-dihydro-3-methyl-2H-1,4-benzoxazine); […]quintocet-mexyl ((5-chloroquinolin-8-yloxy)acetic acid); cy[…]metrinil ((Z)-cyanomethoxyimino(phenyl)acetonitrile); cyprosulfamide (N-[4-(cyclopropylcarbamoyl)phenylsulfonyl]-o-anisami[…]); dichlormid (N, N-diallyl-2, 2-dichloroacetamide); dicyclonon ((RS)-1-dichloroacety[…]3,8a-trimethylperhydropyrrolo[1,2-c]pyrimidin-6-o[…]); dietholate (O,O-diethyl O-phenyl phosphorothioate); fenchlorazole-ethyl (1-(2,4-dichlorophen[…]-5-trichloromethyl-1H-1,2,4-triazole-3-carboxylic acid); fenclorim (6-dichloro-2-phenylpyrimidine); flurazole ([…]nzyl 2-chloro-4-trifluoromethyl-1,3-thiazole-5-carboxylate); fluxofenim (4′-chloro-2,2,2-trifl[…]roacetophenone (EZ)—O-1,3-dioxolan-2-ylmethyloxime); isoxadifen (4,5-dihydro-5,5-diphenyl-1,2-oxazole-3-carboxylic acid); mefenpyr ((RS)-1-(2,4-dic[…]rophenyl)-5-methyl-2-pyrazoline-3,5-dicarbo[…]lic acid); mephenate (4-ch[…]ophenyl methylcarbamate); MG 191; naphthalic anhydride; oxabetri[…] ((Z)-1,3-dioxolan-2-ylmethoxyimino(phenyl)acetonitrile); isoxadi[…] (4,5-dihydro-5,5-diphenyl-1,2-oxazole-3-carboxylic acid); cyprosulfamide; salts and esters thereof, and mixtures thereof.

35-44. (canceled)

45. The composition of claim 1, wherein the composition further comprise at least one co-herbicide and wherein the

Fig. 2.2 Identification strategy
Source: SureChEMBL database

Number of Newly Invented Compounds in Patent Claims Each compound listed in patent claims can be known to the state of the art (i.e. previously claimed along with other chemical compounds) or introduced for the first time in a chemical patent. In this case, the sought of the intellectual property protection by firms cover a complete brand-new chemical space in which all the combinations (i.e. the new compounds along with other compounds) result to be new for the state of the art. Hence, a set of newly invented compounds in a patent indicate the firm's search activity in within the chemical space and the intent to protect a completely new region of chemical space. Thus, the number of newly invented patented compounds provides a fine-grained representation of the intensity of the firm's search efforts and can proxy innovation novelty.

2.4.2 Difference-in-Differences Estimation

Difference-in-differences (DID) estimations are used to study the role of interventions like economic policies and events in natural experiments. This statistical technique analyses the differential effect of the intervention or treatment on a treatment group and compares it to a control group that is not exposed to the treatment (Angrist and Pischke 2009). A common experimental setup is observing two groups over two-time periods, where the first group is exposed to treatment in the second-time period, while the control group is not exposed to the treatment the entire period. To eliminate biases in second-time period comparisons due to trends or inherent differences, the average gains in the control group are subtracted from the average gain in the treatment group.

To estimate only the effect of the Stockholm Convention on the number of chemical compounds patented and in the number of newly invented chemical compounds using a difference-in-differences approach, I rely on control set of unregulated chemical patents sharing similar characteristics but not impacted by Stockholm Convention.

2.4.3 Control Group

To investigate whether and to what extent the increase in compound patenting as well as the increase in the newly invented compounds of POP-related patents is a mirror of an increase in the compound increase of patents that share similar characteristics (except disclosing POPs in patent claims) I rely on a control group. The control group is generated through the exact matching of some observable characteristics such as the filing year, the IPC class (four digit), the granting status and the application through PCT (Patent Convention Treaty).

For the difference-indifferences estimation, I focus on subset POP-related patents. Countries can differ in access to new technologies, scientific and human resources and organizational cultures. To control for these exogenous factors that could bias the analysis, I select only patent application filed through PCT (Patent Convention Treaty) filed at the European Patent Office (EPO). The European Union played a pivotal role in the Stockholm Convention as it was one of the promoters and decided to implement the convention by eliminating the use of POPs rather than restricting it. Similarly, the control group is also comprised of patents filed at the EPO. The European Union is also the second worldwide largest market for chemicals, and firms interested in this market would typically file patents here (Ahuja and Morris Lampert 2001). Restricting the sample to the EPO patents maintains consistency, reliability and comparability in factors like accessibility to chemistry technologies and resources needed for technological search. For each POP-related patent, I match up to two controls with the described similar characteristics and no POP in their claims. For 322 POP-related patents, I identify 852 control patents.

2.4.4 Model

The generic difference-in-differences (DID) model is specified as:

$$y = \beta_0 + \beta_1 B + \delta_0 d2 + \delta_1 d2.dB + u$$

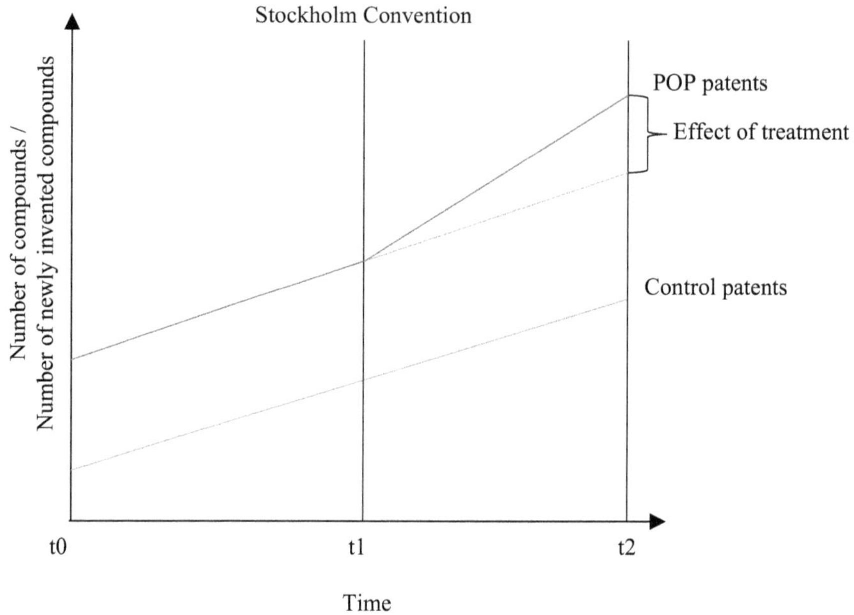

Fig. 2.3 Experimental setup to test the effect of the Stockholm Convention on the number of patented compounds and on the number of newly invented compounds
Source: Author own elaboration
Legend t0–t1 = pre-intervention period (1991–2000) t1 = intervention (2001 Stockholm Convention) t1–t2 = post-intervention period (2001–2010)

where *y* is the outcome variable (number of patented compounds/number of patented newly invented compounds), *d2* is a dummy variable for the second-time period (post-Stockholm Convention), the dummy variable *dB* captures differences between treatment and control groups before the second time period (treatment). The coefficient of interest is *δ1d2.dB*. The difference-in-differences estimate is:

$$\delta_1 = \left(y_{B,2} - y_{B,1}\right) - \left(y_{A,2} - y_{A,1}\right)$$

Therefore, estimation of Stockholm Convention effect = (POP compounds – control compounds) post-Convention – (POP compounds – control compounds) post-Convention (Fig. 2.3).

2.4.5 Results

Changes in firm patenting activity are shown in Figs. 2.4, 2.5 and 2.6. In Fig. 2.4, number of firms between 1991 and 2010 goes up exponentially indicating an increase in firms engaged in POP-related patent activities. Figure 2.5 shows an increase in firm patenting between 1991 and 2010. To capture the rate of inventive activity among chemical firms, I calculated an average score (total patents per year/

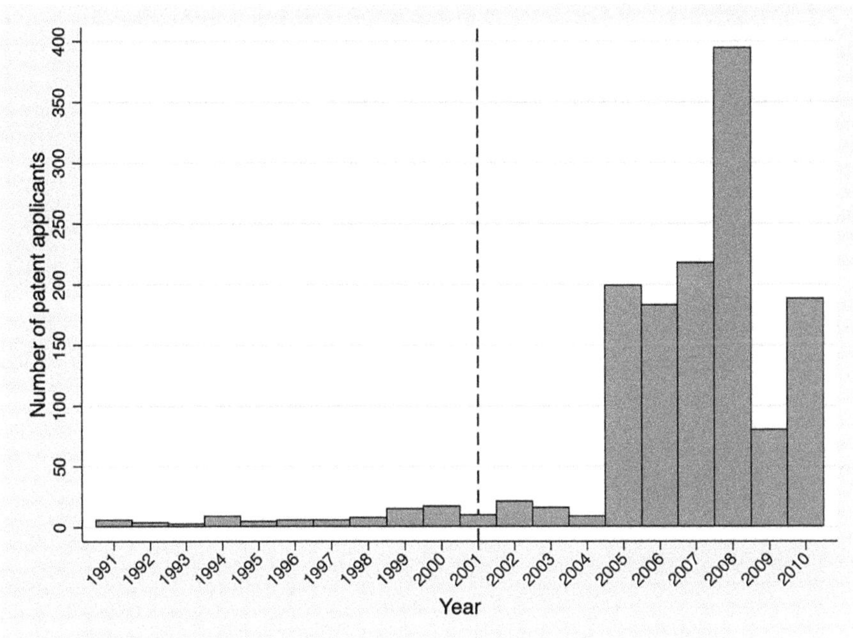

Fig. 2.4 Number of POP patent applicants by year
Source: Author's own elaboration

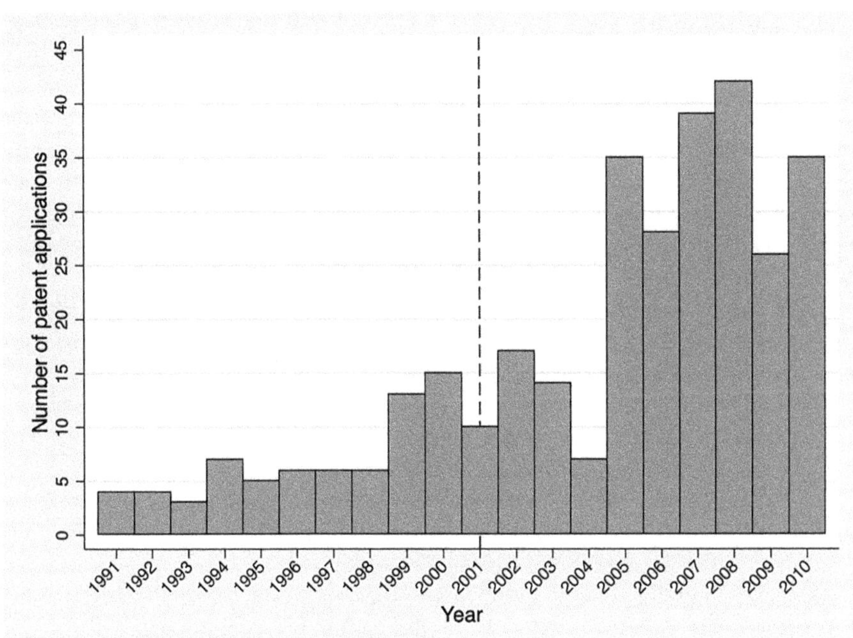

Fig. 2.5 Number of patent POP patent application by year
Source: Author's own elaboration

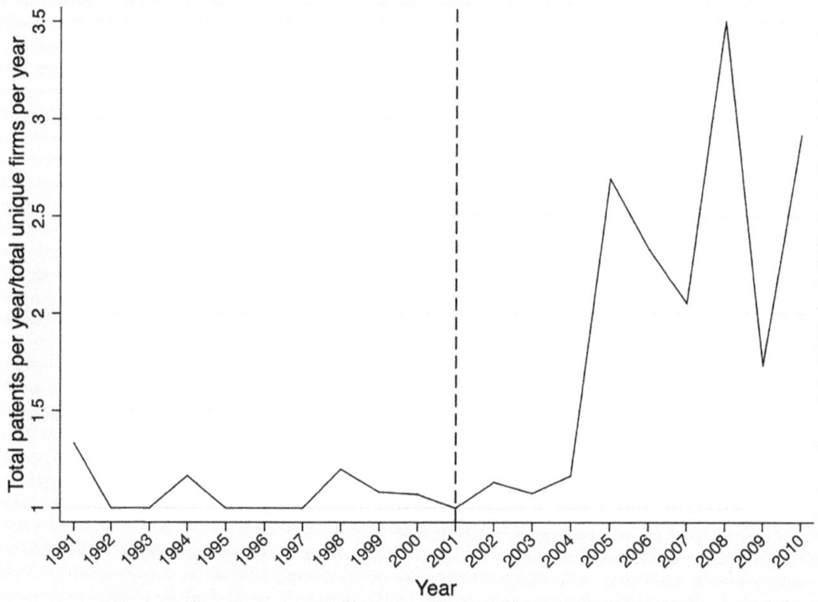

Fig. 2.6 Patents per year/firms per year
Source: Author's own elaboration

total unique firms per year) to account for the overall industry inventive activity across time. The trend line is shown in Fig. 2.6 where I observe steep increase over the 10-year time period which followed the signature of the Stockholm Convention. In sum, after the Stockholm Convention, I observe more patenting activity, a greater number of firms engaged in POP-related patents and overall inventive activity increasing across the industry (Figs. 2.4, 2.5 and 2.6), thus supporting Hypothesis 1(a).

Figure 2.7 shows the number of compounds for POP-related patents and control patents. The widening of the gap between the two becomes more pronounced after the signature of the Stockholm Convention in 2001.

Figure 2.8 points out an interesting trend – the number of compounds per patents is consistently higher for POP-related patents, and the gap between treated and controls widens after the Stockholm Convention.

Figure 2.9 shows the number of newly invented compounds for POP-related patents and control patents. Even in this case, the widening of the gap between the two after the signature of the Stockholm Convention becomes more pronounced.

Figure 2.10 shows that the number of newly invented compounds per patents is consistently higher for POP-related patents, and the gap between treated and controls widens after the Stockholm Convention.

Tables 2.1 and 2.2 show descriptive statistics and results for the difference-in-differences estimation. In Model 1, the difference-in-differences estimator (*POP#POST_BAN*) is calculated using ordinary least squares (OLS) regression with firm fixed effects and the standard errors clustered for robustness at firm level

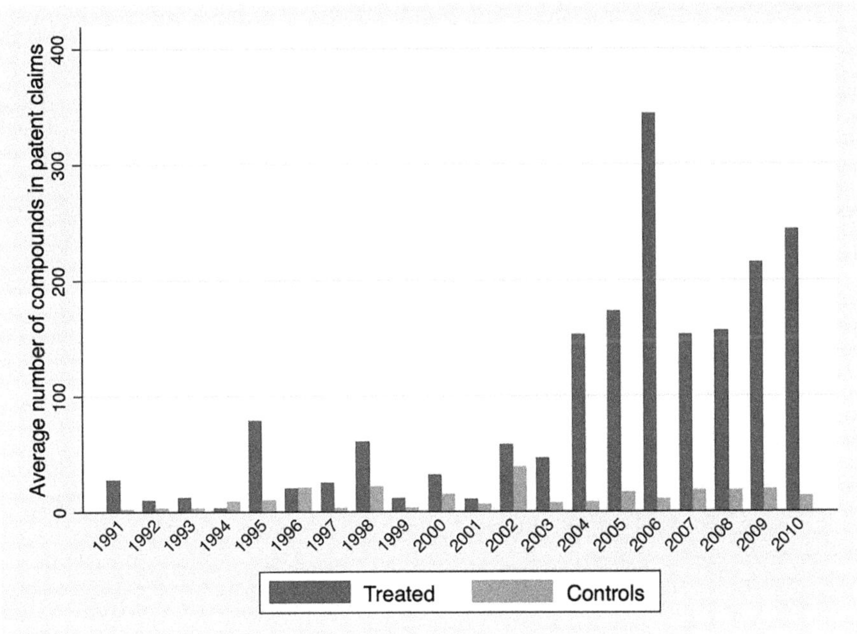

Fig. 2.7 Evolution of patented compounds (treated and controls)
Source: Author's own elaboration

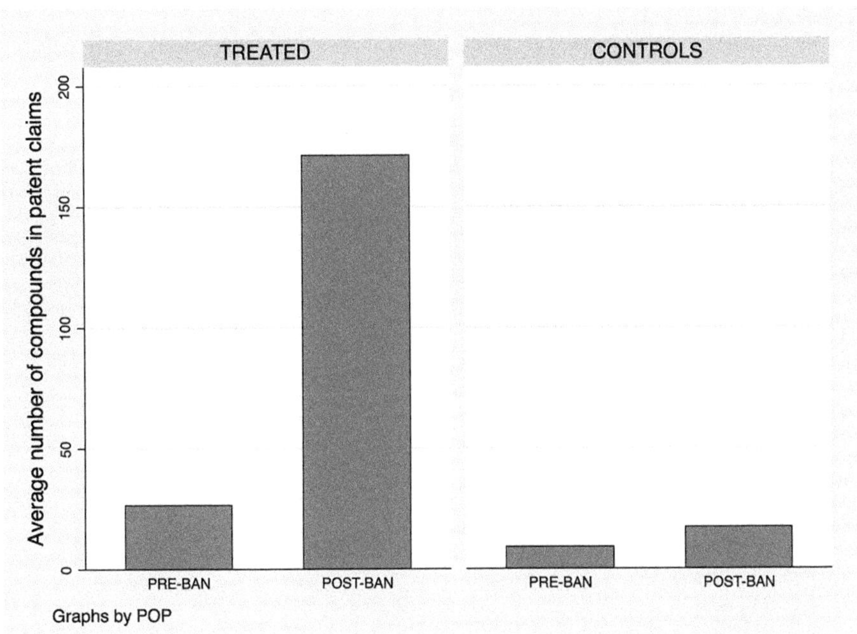

Fig. 2.8 Average number of patented compounds (treated and controls)
Source: Author's own elaboration

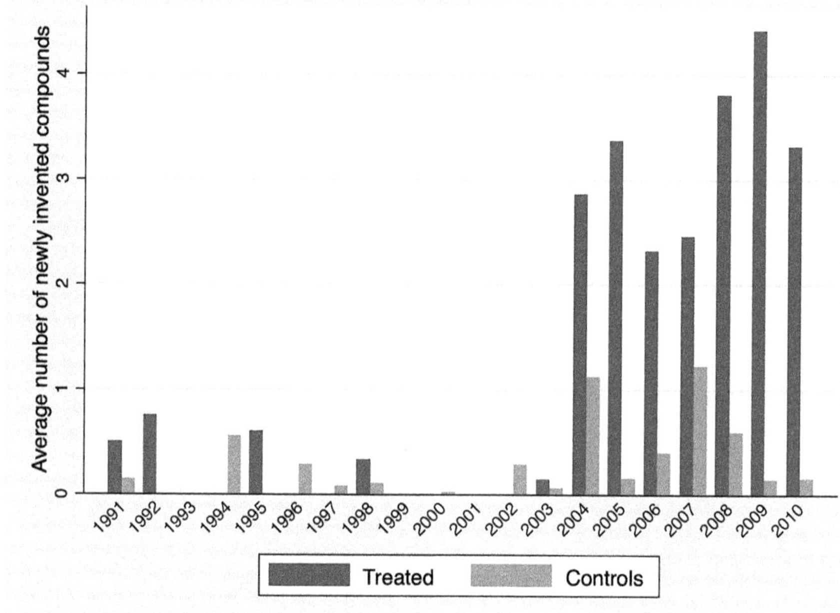

Fig. 2.9 Evolution of newly invented patented compounds (treated and controls)
Source: Author's own elaboration

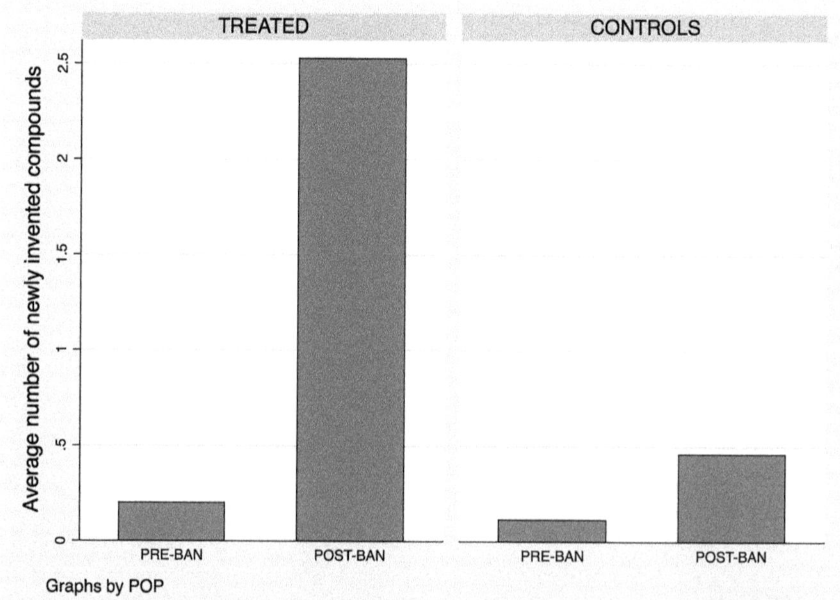

Fig. 2.10 Average number of newly invented patented compounds (treated and controls)
Source: Author's own elaboration

Table 2.1 Descriptive statistics for treated and controls

	Treated	Controls
Patent priority application country	European patent office (EPO)	European patent office (EPO)
Time period	1991–2000	2001–2010
Observations	322	852
Compounds in patent claims	Min: 1	Min: 1
	Max: 6287	Max: 462
	Mean: 145.87	Mean: 15.28
	Std. dev.: 386.47	Std. dev.: 37.49
Newly invented compounds in patent claims	Min: 0	Min: 1
	Max: 107	Max: 99
	Mean: 2.18	Mean: 0.39
	Std. dev.: 7.09	Std. dev.: 3.80

Source: Author's own elaboration

Table 2.2 Difference-in-differences estimates for the effect of the Stockholm Convention on the number of patented compounds and on the number of newly invented compound

Variables	OLS fixed effects		OLS	OLS fixed effects
Treatment period	*2001*			
	No. of compounds		*No. of newly invented compounds*	
	(1)	*(2)*	*(3)*	*(4)*
POP#POST_BAN	89.98***	153.65***	1.23**	2.36***
	(24.82)	(31.16)	(0.68)	(0.54)
POST_BAN	−20.29***	6.84	−0.04*	0.35**
	(6.34)	(17.09)	(0.37)	(0.17)
POP	8.76**	14.92	0.25*	0.01*
	(3.74)	(27.29)	(0.59)	(0.09)
Constant	−5.10**	9.83	−0.29	0.11**
	(1.99)	(15.25)	(0.33)	(0.06)
Observations	1174	1174	1174	1174
R-squared	0.1751	0.1045	0.0179	0.0412
Treatment period	*2004*			
	No. of compounds		*No. of newly invented compounds*	
	(5)	*(6)*	*(7)*	*(8)*
POP#POST_BAN_1	103.23***	163.66***	1.82***	2.74***
	(11.37)	(33.65)	(0.60)	(0.65)
POST_BAN_1	−24.11***	3.10	0.04	0.24
	(6.11)	(2.77)	(0.32)	(0.20)
POP	10.58	26.55***	0.03	0.04
	(9.18)	(7.59)	(0.48)	(0.17)
Constant	−4.70	13.15***	−0.35	0.22**

(continued)

Table 2.2 (continued)

Variables	OLS fixed effects		OLS	OLS fixed effects
	(5.06)	(2.30)	(0.26)	(0.08)
Observations	1174	1174	1174	1174
R-squared	0.1977	0.1146	0.0255	0.0487

Source: Author's own elaboration

Legend

POP: Dummy for treatment (1 = POP patents)

POST_BAN: Dummy for post-intervention period (1 = post-2001)

POP#POST_BAN: Interaction term for treatment and post-intervention period (diff-in-diff estimator)

POST_BAN_1: Dummy for post-intervention period (1 = post-2004)

POP#POST_BAN_1: Interaction term for treatment and post-intervention period (diff-in-diff estimator)

Note: ***$p < 0.01$, **$p < 0.05$, *$p < 0.1$. Robust standard errors in parentheses. Standard errors clustered at firm level

for the intervention time period 2001. The difference-in-difference estimate for the effect of the 2001 signature of the Stockholm Convention is 89.98. To check whether these effects are consistent even after the ratification of the Stockholm Convention, Model 5 measures the effect for the 2004 intervention period. Results are similar and statistically significant. This implies that controlling for the independent effect of similar and unregulated chemical inventions (i.e. the Control patents), POP-related patents accounted nearly for 90 more compounds for each patent. These results are statistically significant and consistent with Models 2 and 6 (run without fixed effects). This implies that the Stockholm Convention increased compound output by 90 compounds per patent after the signature of the Stockholm Convention (2001) and by 160 compounds per patent after the ratification of the Stockholm Convention (2004).

As for the number of newly invented compounds, Model 3 estimates for the effect of the 2001 signature of the Stockholm Convention, while Model 7 measures the effects of the ratification of the Convention in 2004 using ordinary least squares (OLS) regression with firm fixed effects and the standard errors clustered for robustness at firm level. Results are statistically significant and consistent with Models 4 and 8 (run without fixed effects) suggesting that the Stockholm Convention increased the number of newly invented compounds by 2 compounds per patent in after the 2001 intervention period and by 4 compounds per patent after the 2004 intervention period. Coupled, these results support Hypothesis 1(b).

2.5 Conclusions

Persistent organic pollutants are the first chemicals to be globally banned by the 2001 Stockholm Convention. Attention to their noxious impact has only recently revamped because of their re-volatilization tied to climate change. However, while the environmental regulation was designed to forbid future production and use of these chemicals, it did not directly regulate the R&D processes underpinning the banned technologies, perhaps based on the presumption that these would have been phased out too. Using a novel dataset of chemical patent applications, I find that environmental regulation as the Stockholm Convention is correlated with an increase in the number of chemical patents, chemical compounds disclosed in patent claims and in the number of newly invented compounds. These findings point to the role of environmental regulation as catalysts in knowledge recombination, focusing search processes and enabling firms to explore more of the technological landscapes. While most extant research point out the role of environmental regulations on the invention of new or improved product processes, there has been no systematic empirical analysis of the processes of search and innovation on existing and regulated technologies. Throughout this study, I tried to open the black box of chemical inventions using a novel dataset of existing and potentially polluting inventions that have not been used previously in management research. I proposed that the environmental regulation facilitated the search and innovation making compound production more intensive – resulting in more inventive activity. The results support hypotheses 1a and 1b.

These results also support prior studies on the role of environmental regulation and technical change. By showing a significant effect on the production of compounds in the time period 1991–2010, these results empirically support theoretical models on the role of environmental regulations on exploration and innovation. The significant effect of the Convention on compound patenting and the increase in the newly invented compounds support prior work on the idea that environmental regulations accelerate the rate and intensity of technological innovation.

Along these lines, the environmental regulation as the Stockholm Convention acts as a form of complementary asset that allowed firms to change their innovation strategies (Teece 1986). The separate effect of the Stockholm Convention (i.e. 90 + compound per patent and 2 + newly invented compound per patent) is supported by the difference-in-difference estimations controlling for the effect of similar technologies.

From a policy perspective, this result is interesting as the environmental regulation shows a stronger and separate effect on compound patenting and newly invented compound production. This is due to the fact that the regulation opens up new and unexplored territories in chemical field. Thus, regulatory efforts aimed at protecting humans and ecosystems from polluting technologies led to more exploration of chemical space and increased novel compound output per patent – in essence, creating conditions ripe for technological innovation. Understanding the economic impact of environmental regulations and how they influence innovation processes is important for public policy, R&D management and firm strategy. By linking environmental regulations with industry innovation, this empirical analysis sheds new light on important but largely unexplored questions in the literature on technological search. These results reveal an interesting finding: environmental regulations not only increase the rate of invention but also impact the nature of technological search and underlying strategies, suggesting that regulations can enhance the quality of industry innovation.

References

Ahuja, Gautam, and Curba Morris Lampert. 2001. Entrepreneurship in the large corporation: A longitudinal study of how established firms create breakthrough inventions. *Strategic Management Journal* 22 (6–7): 521–543. https://doi.org/10.1002/smj.176.

Angrist, Joshua, and Jorn-Steffen Pischke. 2009. *Mostly harmless econometrics: An empiricist's companion*. Princeton: Princeton University Press.

Ansari, Shahzad, Frank Wijen, and Barbara Gray. 2013. Constructing a climate change logic: An institutional perspective on the "tragedy of the commons". *Organization Science* 24 (4): 1014–1040.

Bates, Edward. 2008. Avoiding legal obligations created by human rights treaties. *The International and Comparative Law Quarterly* 57 (4): 751–788.

Bekkers, Rudi, Arianna Martinelli, and Federico Tamagni. 2020. The impact of including standards-related documentation in patent prior art: Evidence from an EPO policy change. *Research Policy* 49 (7): 104007. https://doi.org/10.1016/j.respol.2020.104007.

DiMasi, J.A., L. Feldman, A. Seckler, and A. Wilson. 2010. Trends in risks associated with new drug development: Success rates for investigational drugs. *Clinical Pharmacology and Therapeutics* 87 (3): 272–277. https://doi.org/10.1038/clpt.2009.295.

Dosi, Giovanni. 1982. Technological paradigms and technological trajectories: A suggested interpretation of the determinants and directions of technical change. *Research Policy* 11 (3): 147–162.

Drews, J. 2000. Drug discovery: A historical perspective. *Science* 287 (5460): 1960–1964. https://doi.org/10.1126/science.287.5460.1960.

Fitzgerald, L., and D.S. Wikoff. 2014. Persistent organic pollutants. In *Encyclopedia of toxicology*, ed. Philip Wexler, 3rd ed., 820–825. Oxford: Academic Press.

Fleming, Lee, and Olav Sorenson. 2004. Science as a map in technological search. *Strategic Management Journal* 25 (8–9): 909–928. https://doi.org/10.1002/smj.384.

Hardin, G. 1968. The tragedy of the commons. *Science* 162 (3859): 1243–1248. https://doi.org/10.1126/science.162.3859.1243.

Hart, Oliver, and Luigi Zingales. 2017. *Companies should maximize shareholder welfare not market value*. ECGI-Finance Working Paper (521).

Henderson, Rebecca, and Iain Cockburn. 1996. Scale, scope, and spillovers: The determinants of research productivity in drug discovery. *RAND Journal of Economics* 27 (1): 32–59.

Hicks, John. 1963. *The theory of wages*. London: Springer.

Jaffe, Adam. 1986. Technological opportunity and spillovers of R&D: Evidence from firms' patents, profits, and market value. *American Economic Review* 76 (5): 984–1001.

Jaffe, Adam, and Manuel Trajtenberg. 1999. International knowledge flows: Evidence from patent citations. *Economics of Innovation and New Technology* 8 (1–2): 105–136.

Jaffe, Adam, Manuel Trajtenberg, and Rebecca Henderson. 1993. Geographic localization of knowledge spillovers as evidenced by patent citations. *The Quarterly Journal of Economics* 108 (3): 577–598.

Jayaraj, Sebastian, and Michelle Gittelman. 2018. Impact of scientific maps on technological search and novelty. *Academy of Management Proceedings* 2018 (1): 15414. https://doi.org/10.5465/ambpp.2018.234.

Kodavanti, P.R.S., J.E. Royland, and K.R.S. Sambasiva Rao. 2014. Toxicology of persistent organic pollutants. In *Reference module in biomedical sciences*. Elsevier, Amsterdam.

Kuhn, Jeffrey M., and Neil C. Thompson. 2019. How to measure and draw causal inferences with patent scope. *International Journal of the Economics of Business* 26 (1): 5–38.

Ma, Jianmin, Hayley Hung, Chongguo Tian, and Roland Kallenborn. 2011. Revolatilization of persistent organic pollutants in the Arctic induced by climate change. *Nature Climate Change* 1 (5): 255.

March, James G. 1991. Exploration and exploitation in organizational learning. *Organization Science* 2 (1): 71–87.

Marco, Alan C., Joshua D. Sarnoff, and Charles A.W. deGrazia. 2019. Patent claims and patent scope. *Research Policy* 48 (9): 103790. https://doi.org/10.1016/j.respol.2019.04.014.

Nelson, Richard R. 2009. *An evolutionary theory of economic change*. Cambridge: Harvard University Press.

Nizzetto, Luca, Matthew Macleod, Katrine Borgå, Ana Cabrerizo, Jordi Dachs, Antonio Di Guardo, Davide Ghirardello, Kaj M. Hansen, Andrew Jarvis, Anders Lindroth, Bernard Ludwig, Donald Monteith, Judith A. Perlinger, Martin Scheringer, Luitgard Schwendenmann, Kirk T. Semple, Lukas Y. Wick, Gan Zhang, and Kevin C. Jones. 2010. Past, present, and future controls on levels of persistent organic pollutants in the global environment. *Environmental Science & Technology* 44 (17): 6526–6531. https://doi.org/10.1021/es100178f.

Papadatos, George, Mark Davies, Nathan Dedman, Jon Chambers, Anna Gaulton, James Siddle, Richard Koks, Sean A. Irvine, Joe Pettersson, and Nicko Goncharoff. 2016. SureChEMBL: A large-scale, chemically annotated patent document database. *Nucleic Acids Research* 44 (D1): D1220–D1228.

Rigét, Frank, Anders Bignert, Birgit Braune, Maria Dam, Rune Dietz, Marlene Evans, Norman Green, Helga Gunnlaugsdóttir, Katrin S. Hoydal, John Kucklick, Robert Letcher, Derek Muir, Stacy Schuur, Christian Sonne, Gary Stern, Gregg Tomy, Katrin Vorkamp, and Simon Wilson. 2019. Temporal trends of persistent organic pollutants in Arctic marine and freshwater biota. *Science of the Total Environment* 649: 99–110. https://doi.org/10.1016/j.scitotenv.2018.08.268.

Scherer, Andreas Georg, and Guido Palazzo. 2011. The new political role of business in a globalized world: A review of a new perspective on CSR and its implications for the firm, governance, and democracy. *Journal of Management Studies* 48 (4): 899–931.

Schilling, Melissa A., and Elad Green. 2011. Recombinant search and breakthrough idea generation: An analysis of high impact papers in the social sciences. *Research Policy* 40 (10): 1321–1331.

Shapiro, Joseph S., and Reed Walker. 2018. Why is pollution from US manufacturing declining? The roles of environmental regulation, productivity, and trade. *American Economic Review* 108 (12): 3814–3854. https://doi.org/10.1257/aer.20151272.

Southall, Noel T., and Ajay. 2006. Kinase patent space visualization using chemical replacements. *Journal of Medicinal Chemistry* 49 (6): 2103–2109. https://doi.org/10.1021/jm051201m.

Teece, David J. 1986. Profiting from technological innovation: Implications for integration, collaboration, licensing and public policy. *Research Policy* 15 (6): 285–305. https://doi.org/10.1016/0048-7333(86)90027-2.

Chapter 3
Are We Moving Towards a More Sustainable World? Insights from Patent Analysis of Chemical Inventions

Abstract Industrialized economies have historically maintained the hope that the advances in science, technology and innovation would have offered to humanity a wide range of options to improve its well-being and attain sustained economic growth. The transition towards a high technological frontier arising from the rapid advances of science, technology and innovation has opened a debate on the relations between innovation-induced industrial activities, related possible social and environmental threats and the role of policies to keep up with industry developments. To investigate those relations, I collect a unique dataset that includes patent applications in chemical technologies and analyse their disclosed groups of compounds by combining patent analysis with computational chemistry, and I develop a novel methodology to measure patent toxicity, that is, the extent to which a patent includes 'components' (i.e. chemical compounds) that are potentially toxic to humans and/or the environment. To illustrate the proposed methodology, I analyse the toxicity of 12 regulated chemical technologies as the persistent organic pollutants (POPs) in comparison with a control group of unregulated technologies. The measurement of patent toxicity opens up interesting avenues for future research and for policy.

3.1 Introduction

There is a lot to worry about climate change, but bioscientists have one specific concern: the revolatilization of persistent organic pollutants (POPs) following the melting of polar ice (Nizzetto et al. 2010; Ma et al. 2011; Rigét et al. 2019). POPs are defined as 'chemical substances that persist in the environment, bio-accumulate through the food chain, and pose a risk of causing adverse effects to human health and the environment' (Fitzgerald and Wikoff 2014). The reason why there is so much concern about their revolatilization in the atmosphere is that they are highly hazardous: they cause cancer, damage the immune and nervous systems and are highly poisonous for human beings, animal species and the environment at large (Kodavanti et al. 2014). For this reason, following the recommendation of the

G. Biggi, *Industrial Dynamics and Firm Strategies in the Agrochemical Industry*, SpringerBriefs in Economics, https://doi.org/10.1007/978-3-031-52689-3_3

Intergovernmental Forum on Chemical Safety (IFCS) and the International Programme on Chemical Safety (IPCS), a first group of a hazardous POPs, also known as the 'Dirty Dozen' (namely, dieldrin, aldrin, chlordane, DDT, endrin, heptachlor, hexachlorobenzene, mirex, pentachlorobenzene, toxaphene, polychlorinated biphenyls, polychlorinated dibenzo-p-dioxins), were banned, or their use was severely restricted starting from 2001 by an international treaty – the Stockholm Convention. The treaty was signed between 2001 and 2002 by 153 countries worldwide, and it was progressively ratified in the following years (most ratifications occurred between 2001 and 2007; see Table 3.1 for an overview of the bans for each POP).

This global ban has mitigated concerns about these hazardous chemicals at least up until very recently when it became clear that they would re-volatilize in the atmosphere as a consequence of melting Antarctic ice. Yet, while most research has addressed the legacy of POPs, very little is known about their future. Are these chemicals and their knowledge really disappearing? Are companies and other inventing organizations conducting research and development (R&D) programs to make these compounds less hazardous for humanity? More specifically, beside banning use and production, has the Stockholm Convention also contributed to the phase out of POP-related inventions and/or to reduce their toxicity?

Extant evidence on regulatory responses shows that regulatory changes generate an impact on producers which, especially in the context if a strict legal enforcement, tend to phase out the banned product in favour of a safer one (e.g. Shapiro and Walker 2018). In that context, however, we know very little about what companies do in their R&D laboratories, although two scenarios seem highly plausible: first, that the phase out of a product will also lead to a discontinuation of its underlying inventive activities, which means that after a ban we should observe a decline in patents connected to the banned technology and product, or, second scenario, that the inventive activities underpinning a banned technology persist but take a less hazardous direction, which means that the patents connected to the banned technology will not necessarily decline but they will become less 'toxic' over time. Both scenarios are desirable on a public policy perspective because they are signals of a more sustainable transition. Patent toxicity can be used to both assess the impact of public policies and regulatory bans and to examine companies' reactions to such bans and their environmental strategies.

3.2 Method

3.2.1 Measuring the Toxicity of Chemical Compounds

The toxicity of a chemical compound is measured along several dimensions or toxicity endpoints. A compound can be toxic to human health, for example, in terms of mutagenicity, which captures the degree to which the chemical causes cell

Table 3.1 List of the 12 POPs: key information

Chemical	Category	Main uses and applications	Main types of exposure and effects	Treaty action (Stockholm Convention)
Aldrin	Pesticide	Applied to soils to kill termites, grasshoppers, corn rootworm and other insect pests	Humans are mostly exposed to aldrin through dairy products and animal meats	Elimination
Chlordane	Pesticide	Used to control termites and as an insecticide on agricultural crops	Human immune system and human carcinogen	Elimination
Dieldrin	Pesticide	Used to control termites and textile pests	Long-term exposures have been associated with chronic health effects	Elimination
Endrin	Pesticide	Insecticide used on the crops such as cotton and grains, also used to control rodents	Endrin poisoning in humans primarily affects the nervous system. Food contaminated with endrin has caused several clusters of poisonings worldwide, especially affecting children	Elimination
Heptachlor	Pesticide	Used to control soil insects and termites	Possible human carcinogen. Food is the major source of exposure for humans	Elimination
Hexachlorobenzene	Industrial chemical	Used to kill fungi that affect food crops	Crosses the placenta to accumulate in foetal tissues and is transferred in breast milk. Extremely toxic to aquatic creatures. Risk of bioaccumulation in an aquatic species is high	Elimination
Mirex	Industrial chemical	Insecticide mainly used to control fire ants	Effects on organisms combined with its persistence suggest that mirex presents a long-term hazard for the environment	Elimination

(continued)

Table 3.1 (continued)

Chemical	Category	Main uses and applications	Main types of exposure and effects	Treaty action (Stockholm Convention)
Polychlorinated biphenyls (PCBs)	Industrial chemical	Range of compounds used in industry as heat exchange fluids, in electric transformers and capacitors, and as additives in paint, carbonless copy paper and plastics	PCBs are associated with cancer in humans, such as cancer of the liver and biliary tract	No new production, reduced use
Toxaphene	Pesticide	Insecticide used on cotton, cereal grains, fruits, nuts and vegetables, has also been used to control ticks and mites in livestock	Exposure can cause damage to the lungs, nervous system and kidneys and can be fatal	Elimination
DDT	Pesticide	Pesticide used to control insects that spread diseases, such as malaria, and also on crops, especially cotton	Liver effects and carcinogenesis; effects on children's health and development; exposure linked to preterm delivery, reduced birth weight and shortened lactation	Elimination, exception for disease control
Pentachlorobenzene	Byproducts of production of other chemicals	Used in PCB products, in dyestuff carriers, as a fungicide, a flame retardant and as a chemical intermediate. Also produced unintentionally during combustion, thermal and industrial processes and present as impurities in solvents or pesticides	Systemic impairment (thyroid, liver, bone, skin); damage to the kidneys and blood cells and the immune, endocrine, developmental and nervous systems	Reduction and minimization
Polychlorinated dibenzo-p-dioxins and furans (PCDDs/PCDDFs)	Byproducts of production of other chemicals	Produced unintentionally during the manufacture of pesticides, emitted through the burning of waste and in all incomplete combustion	Acute lethality; body weight loss; carcinogenesis; dermal toxicity; fatty liver; genotoxicity	Reduction and minimization

Source: Author's own elaboration

mutations, or carcinogenicity, that is, its potential to cause cancer, or the whole spectrum of human health hazards including the functioning of the immune and neurological systems, liver damage, harm to the endocrine system, etc. (Wallace 2012). Moreover, a chemical compound can be toxic to the ecosystem where toxicity endpoints can range, for example, from bee toxicity (i.e. the extent to which a compound harms the reproduction of bees) to biodegradability, which assesses how fast a compound biodegrades in the environment (for a full list of toxicity endpoints, see the OECD Guidelines for the Testing of Chemical).

There are three ways to evaluate the toxicity of chemical compounds: in vivo experiments which assess the toxicity of a given substance directly on a living organism (e.g. an animal); in vitro experiments which assess toxicity on microorganisms, cells or biological molecules outside a living organism; and in silico experiments which assess toxicity based on computer simulations. Compared to in vivo and in vitro experiments, in silico toxicity analysis is relatively new but is becoming more accepted over time (Hemmerich and Ecker 2020). In silico toxicity analysis relies on 'machine-learning software trained on masses of chemical-safety data which is increasingly considered so good at predicting some kinds of toxicity that it now rivals — and sometimes outperforms expensive animal studies' (Van Noorden 2018, p. 163). In essence, it applies of computational chemistry methods to compare the structural and biological features of a chemical compound with the same or similar compounds whose effects have been established by prior in vivo or in vitro research. It has the advantage of being less costly than the other two methods and of avoiding the ethical problems of in vivo experiments. Because of these advantages, our measure of patent toxicity is based on in silico toxicity assessments.

3.2.2 Measuring Patent Toxicity

In this study, I rely on quantitative structure-activity relationships (QSAR) models to assess the potential toxicity of the compounds extracted from the claims listed in the patent documents.[1] QSAR models are part of the so-called silico toxicology approach; it is a relatively recent approach, but it is increasingly used to predict any potentially undesirable or adverse effects of chemical compounds on human health and the environment, based on compounds' chemical structure (Cherkasov et al. 2014; Zimmerman et al. 2020). These models rely on the relationship between chemical structure and physiological action, so that similar molecular structures are expected to exhibit similar biological activities. Toxicity effects or toxicity endpoints can be measured in quantitative (e.g. LD50: lethal dose to 50% of tested individuals) or qualitative terms, such as binary (e.g. toxic or nontoxic) or ordinary (e.g. low, moderate or high toxicity). In this study, we use VEGA HUB software

[1] I decided to focus on the claim section to account for the extent (i.e. the scope) of the protection sought in a patent document (Bekkers et al. 2020; Kuhn and Thompson 2019; Marco et al. 2019).

(www.vegahub.eu) to predict the toxicity endpoints of chemical compounds. The VEGA HUB software was developed and is maintained by the Istituto di Ricerche Farmacologiche Mario Negri (IRFMN) as an open-source and large-scale library of QSAR models and is optimized following the European Legislation on chemical substances REACH.[2] The inputs for the VEGA HUB software are the international structure compound identifiers, and the output is a complete report containing toxicity endpoints and all the supporting information required for each compound (Benfenati et al. 2013). Based on a series of interviews with experts in toxicology and computational medicinal chemistry, we selected 22 out of 59 QSAR models provided by VEGA HUB, which best assess the two classes of toxicity of interest in this note: toxicity for human health and toxicity for the environment. The 22 selected QSAR models (see Table 3.2 Columns 2 and 3) provide an exhaustive representation of compound potential toxicity. To identify compounds toxic to human health, I consider five toxicity endpoints – mutagenicity, carcinogenicity, teratogenicity, steroidal activity and liver damage – using a total of 17 QSAR models (some endpoints can be tested through more than one model). Similarly, I assess environmental toxicity through five QSAR models to test fish toxicity, algae toxicity, bee toxicity, sludge toxicity and ready biodegradability. Each QSAR model provides a different scale of possible results (e.g. a compound may be classified as mutagenic, suspected mutagenic or non-mutagenic). Based on the advice of toxicology experts, I adopt a conservative approach and, thus, do not consider a compound to be toxic if the model signals that the endpoint toxicity is only 'possible' or 'suspect' (Table 3.2, Column 4). Further details on toxicity endpoints and related QSAR models and their predictions are reported in the Technical Appendix.

Subsequently, I aggregate the chemical compound toxicity scores at the patent level. Chemical patent claims can include a few or several compounds, sometimes several hundreds. These compounds may be active ingredients or other substances needed for to activate the product or process functions (e.g. reagents, catalysts, etc.). In some cases, a single patent could cover more than one active principle: for instance, the well-known commercial crop management product Round-Up, which was produced by Monsanto (now Bayer), includes both glyphosate (a broad-spectrum herbicide) and endosulfan (an insecticide). Patent claims also can include different combinations of active ingredients and other compounds, thus providing alternative 'formulae' for which the patent applicants seek intellectual protection.

My approach to measuring patent toxicity is based exclusively on the toxicity of the individual compounds present in the patent claim. It does not account for their interactions and synergistic or antagonistic effects (see the conclusion to this section).

Total count toxicity (TC_Tox) counts the total number of compounds in the patent claim that are classified as toxic to human health or to the environment. As

[2] The EU regulation REACH (Registration, Evaluation, Authorisation and Restriction of Chemicals) addresses the production and use of chemical substances and their potential impacts on both human health and the environment. In particular, it includes QSAR models as alternative tools for risk assessment of chemical substances.

Table 3.2 QSAR models and toxicity endpoints

(1) Impact on	(2) Toxicity endpoint	(3) QSAR model	(4) Scale of possible results	(5) Criteria for classification
Human health	1. Mutagenicity	CONSENSUS	Mutagenic, non-mutagenic	'Mutagenic' in one or more QSAR
		CAESAR	Mutagenic, suspect mutagenic, non-mutagenic	
		SarPy/IRFMN	Mutagenic, possible non-mutagenic, non-mutagenic	
		ISS	Mutagenic, non-mutagenic	
		KNN/read across	Mutagenic, non-mutagenic, non-predicted	
	2. Carcinogenicity	CAESAR	Carcinogen, non-carcinogen	'Carcinogen' in one or more QSAR
		ISS	Carcinogen, non-carcinogen	
		IRFMN/Antares	Carcinogen, possible non-carcinogen	
		IRFMN/ISSCAN-CGX	Carcinogen, possible non-carcinogen	
		Oral classification IRFMN	Carcinogen, non-carcinogen	
		Inhalation classification IRFMN	Carcinogen, non-carcinogen	
	3. Teratogenicity	CAESAR	Toxicant, non-toxicant	'Toxicant' in one or more QSAR
		PG	Toxicant, non-toxicant	
	4. Steroidal activity	IRFMN	Active, non-active	'Active' in one or more QSAR
		IRFMN/CERAPP	Active, possible active, possible non-active, non-active, not predicted	
		IRFMN/COMPARA	Active, non-active	
	5. Liver damage	IRFMN	Toxic, non-toxic, unknown	'Toxic' in one or more QSAR

(continued)

Table 3.2 (continued)

(1)	(2)	(3)	(4)	(5)
Impact on	Toxicity endpoint	QSAR model	Scale of possible results	Criteria for classification
Environment	1. Fish toxicity	SarPy/IRFMN	Toxic-1 (less than 1 mg/L), Toxic-2 (between 1 and 10 mg/L), Toxic-3 (between 10 and 100 mg/L), non-toxic (more than 100 mg/L)	'Toxic-1 (less than 1 mg/L)', 'Toxic-2 (between 1 and 10 mg/L)', or 'Toxic-3 (between 10 and 100 mg/L)'
	2. Algae toxicity	ProtoQSAR/Combase	Toxic, non-toxic	'Toxic'
	3. Bee toxicity	KNN/IRFMN	Strong toxicity (lower than 1 μg/bee), moderate toxicity (between 1 and 100 μg/bee), low toxicity (over 100 μg/bee), non-predicted	'Strong toxicity (lower than 1 μg/bee)', 'moderate toxicity (between 1 and 100 μg/bee)', or 'low toxicity (over 100 μg/bee)'
	4. Sludge toxicity	ProtoQSAR/Combase	Toxic, non-toxic	'Toxic'
	5. Ready biodegradability	IRFMN	Readily biodegradable, possible readily biodegradable, possible non-readily biodegradable, non-readily biodegradable, not classifiable	'Non-readily biodegradable' or 'possible non-readily biodegradable'

Source: Author own elaboration

already discussed, I separate human health from environmental impacts and measure TC_Tox separately. TC_Tox_HUMAN$_p$ for human health is defined as:

$$\text{TC\_Tox\_HUMAN}_p = \sum_{c=1}^{C} D_c$$

where c ($c = 1, 2, \ldots, C$) are the compounds in patent p and D_c is a dummy variable equal to 1 if the compound c is categorized as toxic according to at least one of the five human toxicity endpoints (i.e. mutagenicity, carcinogenicity, teratogenicity, steroidal activity, liver damage). TC_Tox_ENV_p for the environment is defined as:

$$\text{TC}_{\text{Tox\_ENV}\,p} = \sum_{c=1}^{C} D_c$$

where c ($c = 1, 2, \ldots, C$) are the compounds in patent p and Dc is a dummy variable equal to 1 if the compound c is categorized as toxic according to at least one of the five human environmental endpoints (i.e. fish toxicity, algae toxicity, bee toxicity, sludge toxicity, ready biodegradability) for environmental impacts.

Share toxicity (S_Tox) is measured as the share of the patent claim's compounds that are classified as toxic either to human health or to environment, over the total number of compounds disclosed in the claim. Hence, I define the following measures:

$$\text{S\_Tox\_HUMAN}_p = \frac{\text{TC\_Tox\_HUMAN}_p}{C}$$

$$\text{S\_Tox\_ENV}_p = \frac{\text{TC\_Tox\_ENV}_p}{C}$$

where C is the number of compounds reported in patent p.

Endpoint toxicity (E_Tox) is measured as the total number of toxicity endpoints detected on either human health or the environment, over the total possible number of toxicity endpoints in the patent.

$$\text{E\_Tox\_HUMAN}_p = \frac{\sum_{c=1}^{C}\sum_{e=1}^{E} D_{c,e}}{C * 5}$$

$$e = \{\text{mutagenicity,carcinogenicity,teratogenicity,steroidal activity,and liver damage}\}$$

$$\mathrm{E\_Tox\_ENV}_p = \frac{\sum_{c=1}^{C}\sum_{e=1}^{E} D_{c,e}}{C*5}$$

$$e = \{\text{fish toxicity,algae toxicity,bee toxicity,sludge toxicity,ready biodegradability}\}$$

where patent p includes c compounds ($c = 1,2, \ldots, C$) and $D_{c,e}$ is a dummy variable equal to 1 if the compound c is toxic for the endpoint e. The normalization is based on the theoretical maximum (i.e., 5* C).[3]

Toxicity concentration (C_Tox) measures the extent to which toxicity is concentrated in one or a few compounds or is detected equally across all the patented compounds, based on an adaptation to the Herfindahl-Hirschman Index (HHI). The two measures of toxicity concentration related to human health (C_Tox_HUMAN_p) and to the environment (C_Tox_ENV_p) are defined as follows:

$$C_{\mathrm{Tox\_HUMAN}\,p} = \sum_{c=1}^{C}\left(\frac{\sum_{c=1}^{C}\sum_{e=1}^{E} D_{c,e}}{\mathrm{TOT}_{\mathrm{END}_{\mathrm{HUM}}}}\right)^2$$

$$e = \{\text{mutagenicity,carcinogenicity,teratogenicity,steroidal activity,liver damage}\}$$

$$\mathrm{C\_Tox\_ENV}_p = \sum_{c=1}^{C}\left(\frac{\sum_{c=1}^{C}\sum_{e=1}^{E} D_{c,e}}{\mathrm{TOT\_END\_ENV}}\right)^2$$

$$e = \{\text{fish toxicity,algae toxicity,bee toxicity,sludge toxicity,ready biodegradability}\}$$

where patent p includes c compounds ($c = 1,2, \ldots, C$) and $D_{c,e}$ is a dummy variable equal to 1 if the compound c is toxic for the endpoint e. TOT_END_HUM and

[3] For instance, consider the patent p disclosing compounds A and B in the claims section. Compound A is shown to be toxic for mutagenicity, carcinogenicity, teratogenicity, steroidal activity and liver damage endpoints, scoring 5 in the human health toxicity class. Compound B is shown to be toxic for the carcinogenicity endpoint, scoring 1 in the human health toxicity class. As the total detected endpoints for patent p are 6 over two compounds, E_Tox_HUMAN_p is calculated as 6/(2*5) = 0.6 where (2*5) = 10 is the 'theoretical' maximum, indicating that the patent is toxic for all the endpoints in the human health toxicity category.

TOT_END_ENV are the total numbers of human toxicity endpoints and environmental toxicity endpoints, respectively, detected in patent *p*.[4]

3.3 Application of the Method

3.3.1 Patent Search

In this study, I rely on two main databases: the chemical database of the European Molecular Biology Laboratory (SureChEMBL) and the EPO-PATSTAT. SureChEMBL is a publicly available large-scale database (Papadatos et al. 2016) which has the unique feature of providing comprehensive compound-patent association maps and includes information indicating the chemical compounds extracted from a specific section of a specific patent document such as the title, abstract, claims or the patent text. The SureChEMBL database provides also information on chemical compound international identifiers (i.e. ChEMBL identifier, SMILES, standard InChIKey) that allow to precisely search all the patents related to a specific compound. To retrieve all the patents associated with each POP, I use one or multiple CAS Registry Number identifiers (see Table 3.3 for the details of the search strategy). Most importantly, the SureChEMBL database allows us to identify all patents that cite a POP in its claims, which are the extent (i.e. the scope) of the protection sought in a patent application (Bekkers et al. 2020; Kuhn and Thompson 2019; Marco et al. 2019).

The search in SureChEMBL identifies 1113 POP-related patent applications at European Patent Office (EPO), US Patent Office (USPTO), Japan Patent Office (JPO) and World Intellectual Property Organization (WIPO) between 1991 and 2010. I decided to focus on patent applications because they give a window onto the exploratory efforts of assignees, unlike granted patent, which only represent a small percentage of the filed applications. Some of the retrieved patent applications might protect the same invention in multiple legislations among the four available in the ChEMBL database. To avoid double or multiple count, I focus our analysis at the unique DOCDB patent family level. I then use the EPO-PATSTAT (version Autumn 2018) database to identify the DOCDB patent families for all the POP-related patent applications retrieved from the ChEMBL database. The final set includes 624 unique DOCDB patent families including 5240 patent applications filed in 75 patent authorities of which 233 (2.52%) related to aldrin, 840 (9.08%) related to

[4] For instance, consider a patent p disclosing compounds A and B in the claim section. Compound A is shown to be toxic for mutagenicity, carcinogenicity, teratogenicity, steroidal activity and liver damage endpoints, thus scoring 5 in the human health toxicity class. Compound B is shown to be toxic for the carcinogenicity endpoint, thus scoring 1 in the human health toxicity class. As the total detected endpoints for patent *p* are 6 across two compounds, C_Tox_HUMAN_p is calculated as $(5/6)^2 + (1/6)^2 = 0.7222$. The result (0.7222) denotes high concentration of human health toxicity due to a higher contribution of compound A.

Table 3.3 POPs-related international chemical identifiers

Chemical	CAS registry number	Molecular formula	SureChEMBL identifier
Aldrin	309-00-2	C12 H8 Cl6	SCHEMBL119263
Chlordane	57-74-9	C10 H6 Cl8	SCHEMBL75811
Dieldrin	60-57-1	C12 H8 Cl6 O	SCHEMBL72829
Endrin	72-20-8	C12 H8 Cl6 O	SCHEMBL72828
Heptachlor	76-44-8	C10 H5 Cl7	SCHEMBL65124
Hexachlorobenzene	118-74-1	C6 Cl6	SCHEMBL26562
Mirex	2385-85-5	C10 Cl12	SCHEMBL118586
Polychlorinated biphenyls (PCBs)	Main 1336-36-3	C12H10−xClx	SCHEMBL2906064
Toxaphene	8001-35-2	C10 H10 Cl8	SCHEMBL5933656
DDT	50-29-3	C14 H9 Cl5	SCHEMBL7181
Pentachlorobenzene	608-93-5	C6 H Cl5	SCHEMBL183144
Polychlorinated dibenzo-p-dioxins and furans (PCDDs/ PCDDFs)	Multiple: 1746-01-6; 40321-76-4; 39227-28-6; 57653-85-7; 19408-74-3; 35822-46-9; 3268-87-9; 51207-31-9; 57117-41-6; 57117-31-4; 70648-26-9; 57117-44-9; 72918-21-9; 60851-34-5; 67562-39-4; 55673-89-7; 39001-02-0	Multiple: C12 H4 Cl4 O2; C12 H3 Cl5 O2; C12 H2 Cl6 O2; C12 H2 Cl6 O2; C12 H2 Cl6 O2; C12 H Cl7 O2; C12 Cl8 O2; C12 H4 Cl4 O; C12 H3 Cl5 O; C12 H3 Cl5 O; C12 H2 Cl6 O; C12 H2 Cl6 O; C12 H2 Cl6 O; C12 H2 Cl6 O; C12 H Cl7 O; C12 H Cl7 O; C12 Cl8 O	SCHEMBL8939; SCHEMBL4170319; SCHEMBL1954279

Source: Author's own elaboration

chlordane, 1044 (11.29%) related to dieldrin, 1072 (11.59%) related to endrin, 759 (8.21%) related to heptachlor, 2348 (25.39%) related to hexachlorobenzene, 328 (3.55%) related to mirex, 29 (0.31%) related to polychlorinated biphenyls (PCBs), 801 (8.66%) related to DDT, 30 (0.32%) related to pentachlorobenzene and 624 (19.07%) related to polychlorinated dibenzo-p-dioxins.

3.3.2 *Control Group*

To test the proposed toxicity indicators, I rely on a control group. The use of a control group will be useful to compare well-known toxic technologies (disclosed in POP-related patents) with technologies for which can be expected low or no toxicity at all.

The control group is generated through the exact matching of some observable characteristics such as the filing year, the IPC class (4 digit), the granting status and the application through PCT (Patent Convention Treaty). To control for these exogenous factors that could bias the analysis, I select only patent application filed through PCT (Patent Convention Treaty) filed at the European Patent Office (EPO). The European Union played a pivotal role in the Stockholm Convention as it was one of the promoters and decided to implement the convention by eliminating the use of POPs rather than restricting it. Similarly, the control group is also comprised of patents filed at the EPO. The European Union is also the second worldwide largest market for chemicals, and firms interested in this market would typically file patents here (Ahuja and Morris Lampert 2001). Restricting the sample to the EPO patents maintains consistency, reliability and comparability in factors like accessibility to chemistry technologies and resources needed for technological search. For each POP-related patent, I match up to two controls with the described similar characteristics and no POP in their claims. For 322 POP-related patents, I identify 852 control patents. Overall, I performed toxicity analyses on 59,995 unique chemical compounds.

3.3.3 Toxicity Analysis Using QSAR Models

I use the VEGA HUB software to run the QSAR models to predict the toxicity endpoints of POP-related patents and control patents. Note that since toxicity was one of the criteria used to select the POP-related patents, its presence is not unexpected. In addition to referring to active substances – our patents – the patent claims include multiple other chemical compounds, such as other active substances, reactants, solvents and catalysts related to the patented chemical process or product. It is not unusual – especially in the pesticide sector – for these other chemical compounds to be as or even more toxic than the key ingredients (Beggel et al. 2010). In this phase I assess the toxicity by considering all the compounds listed in the claim section. Recall that I test five types of toxicity endpoints for each type of impact: (a) mutagenicity, carcinogenicity, teratogenicity, steroidal activity and liver damage for human health impact (for a total of 17 QSAR models) and (b) fish toxicity, algae toxicity, bee toxicity, sludge toxicity and ready biodegradability for environmental impact (5 models).

3.3.4 Patent Toxicity Indicators

I next calculate the above illustrated toxicity indicators for POP-related patents and control patents – total count toxicity (TC_Tox), share toxicity (S_Tox), endpoint toxicity (E_Tox) and toxicity concentration (C_Tox). Note that, in line with current methodologies for predicting the human health and environmental toxicity of chemical compounds, the overall toxicity of a chemical product derives from single-chemical studies (Monosson 2005), which suggests that the presence of at least one toxic chemical compound should be the basis for considering the product described in the invention as toxic.

Figure 3.1a compares the total count toxicity (TC_Tox) indicators for human health contained in a patent by year for treated and control patents. Figure 3.1b reports the same indicator but with reference to environmental toxicity. The two figures suggest similar patterns for human health and environmental toxicity for treated and control patents: the number of toxic compounds is over time higher for POP-related patents suggesting a rapid growth in 2003 even though at a variable rate.

Figure 3.2a reports the share toxicity (S_Tox) indicator for human health contained in a patent by year for treated and control patents. Figure 3.2b reports similar indicator for toxic compounds for the environment. This indicator account for the presence of toxic compounds over total number of compounds disclosed in the patent claims. In both cases, treated and control patents show persistent high level of toxicity share (above 80% for treated patents and 70% for control patents). Jointly considered, total count toxicity and share toxicity show that the upsurge of toxicity of POP-related patents can be ascribed mostly to the increase of patented compounds which result to be toxic according to the QSAR models I used for the toxicity analysis.

Figure 3.3a compares the endpoint toxicity (E_Tox) indicator for human health contained in a patent by year for treated and control patents. Figure 3.3b reports the same indicator but with reference to environmental toxicity. These indicators show the number of predicted endpoints for each toxicity aspects by providing a measure which account for the number of the detected endpoints over the total number of possible endpoints which a patent can disclose. Even in this case, Endpoint toxicity results to be higher for POP-related patents over time (except for 1993 for human health toxicity and 2005 for environmental toxicity) suggesting that treated patents strike far more endpoints than control patents.

Figure 3.4a reports the toxicity concentration (C_Tox) indicator for human health contained in a patent by year for treated and control patents. Figure 3.4b reports similar indicator for toxic compounds for the environment. This indicator measures the extent to which toxicity is concentrated in one or few compounds or it is detected equally across all the patented compounds. Overall, both figures indicate that both in treated and control patents the overall toxicity can be ascribed to the different compounds disclosed in the patent corpus.

This exercise is aimed, primarily, at showing how these indexes function and what they allow for. However, the index values are of interest in their own right since, essentially, they indicate (a) that in most cases the majority of the chemical compounds included in the patent claims are predicted to be toxic to human health (and also but slightly less to the environment) and (b) that toxicity is not concentrated in the active ingredient, which applies, also, to the other compounds.

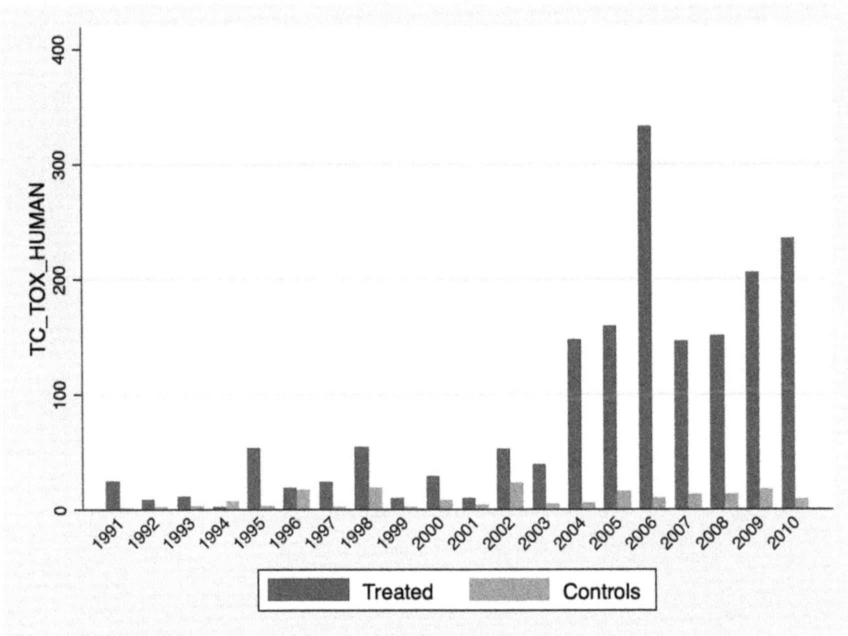

Control

(a)

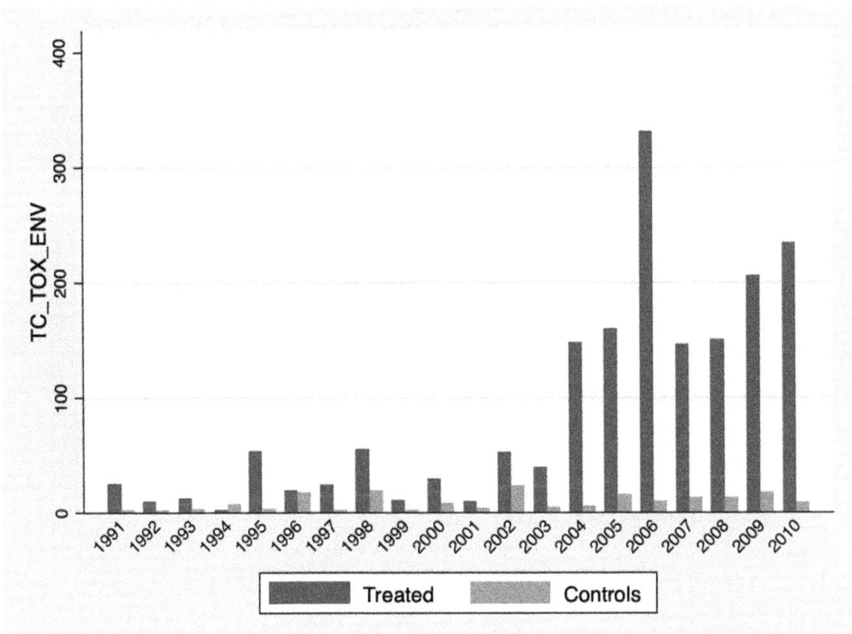

(b)

Fig. 3.1 Evolution of the total count toxicity (TC_TOX) indicators by treated and control
Source: Author's own elaboration

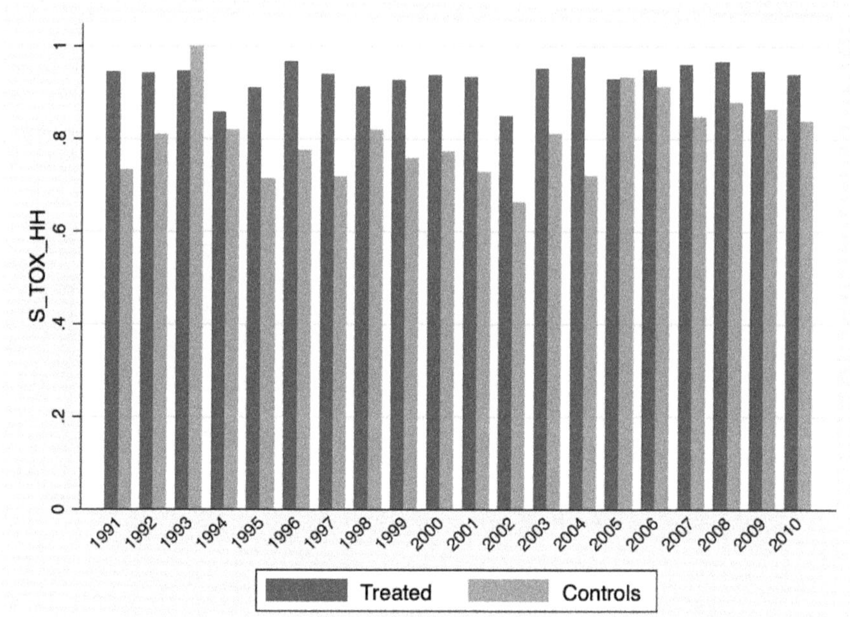

(a)

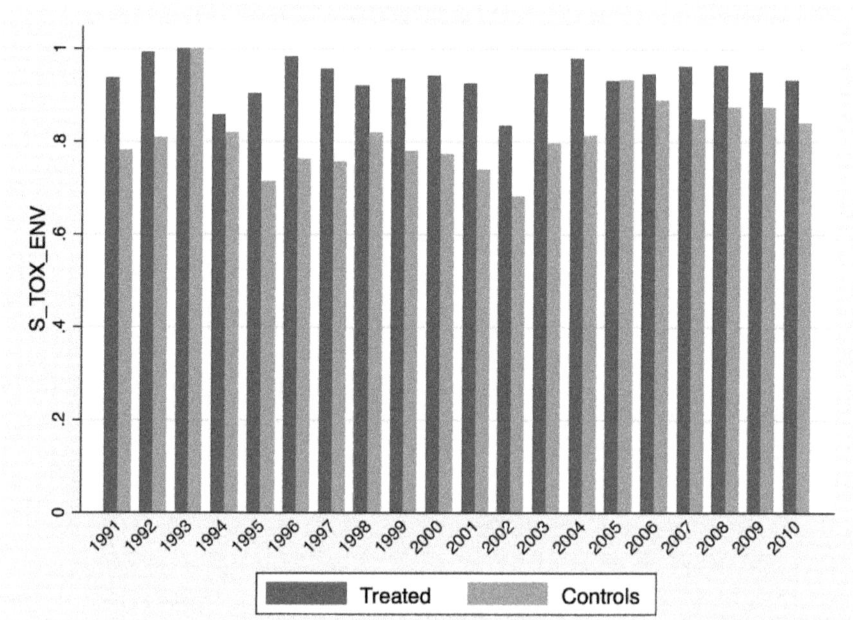

(b)

Fig. 3.2 Evolution of the share toxicity (S_TOX) indicators by treated and control
Source: Author's own elaboration

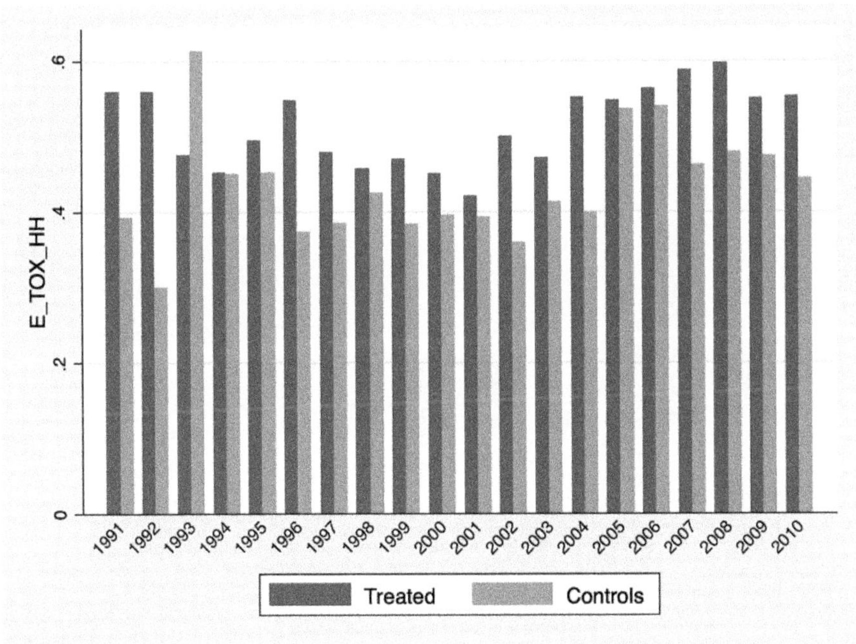

(a)

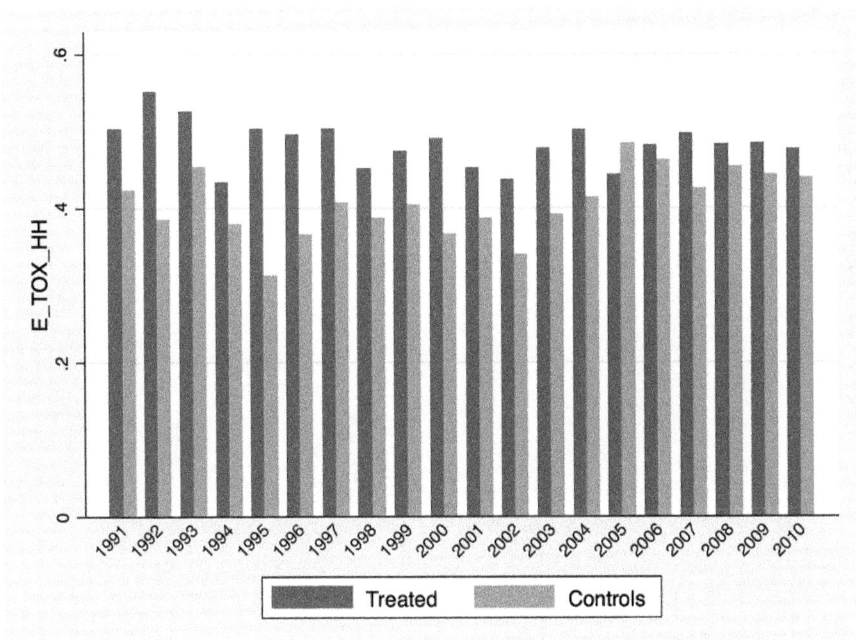

(b)

Fig. 3.3 Evolution of endpoint toxicity (E_TOX) indicators by treated and control
Source: Author's own elaboration

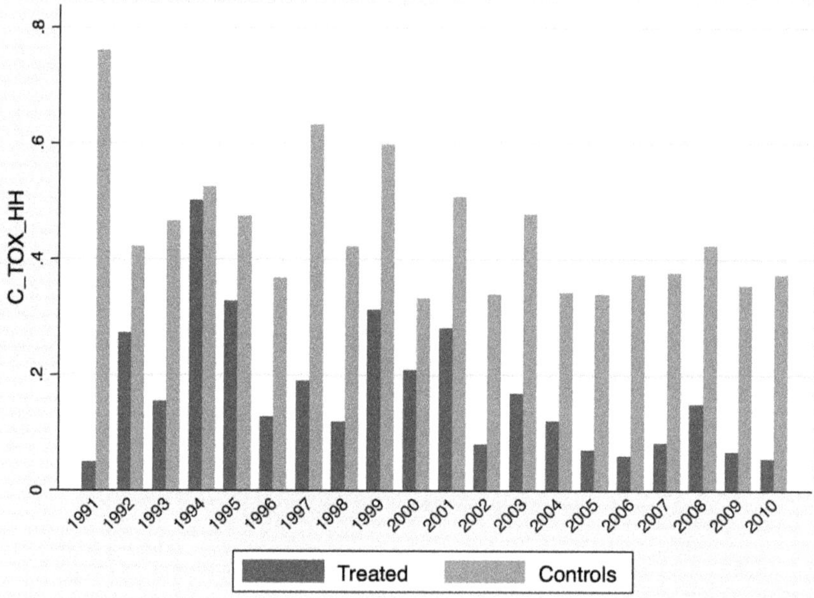

(a)

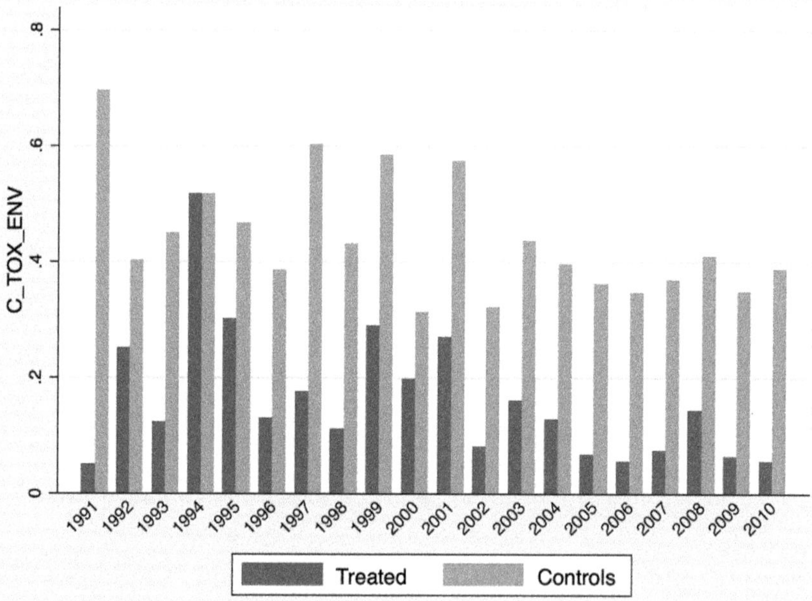

(b)

Fig. 3.4 Evolution of toxicity concentration (C_TOX) indicators by treated and control
Source: Author's own elaboration

3.4 Conclusions

In this study, I combine patent analysis with computational toxicology to formulate a methodological roadmap to guide an investigation of the toxicity of the chemical compounds listed in patent claims, considering 10 toxicity endpoints: (i) mutagenicity, carcinogenicity, teratogenicity, steroidal activity, liver damage for human health impacts and (ii) fish toxicity, algae toxicity, bee toxicity, sludge toxicity and ready biodegradability for environmental impacts. For each type of impact, we proposed four patent toxicity indexes. So far, innovation studies have relied on technological classifications to identify 'good' vs 'bad' innovations, for example, green or brown innovations in the automobile industry (Aghion et al. 2016). I propose a new way to exploit patent information to investigate the technological trajectories of companies and other inventing entities, to assess whether they are investing in the generation of knowledge that is more (or less) likely to lead to a more environmentally and socially sustainable future.

However, our novel approach is only the first step in a bigger and longer-term research agenda. This study suffers from some limitations. First, toxicology research suggests that chemical compounds can cause two types of interactions, such that the combined effect of two or more chemicals can be stronger (additive, synergistic, potentiating, supra-additive) or weaker (antagonistic, inhibitive, sub-additive, infra-additive) than would be expected on the basis of dose addition or response addition (see, e.g. European Commission 2010). This means that the combination of two or more chemical compounds can increase the overall toxicity of the final product or process – as in the case of additive or synergistic effects, for example, or can diminish it – as in the case of antagonistic effects, for example. While additive or synergistic effects are more frequent than antagonist effects, our proposed measures are not able to assess these interactions since computational models that account for the combined impacts of different compounds are not yet available. Moreover, in calculating our indexes, I do not weight each toxic compound by its toxic equivalent factor; this is an issue which requires further developments. Second, our approach uses computational chemistry methods and, therefore, is subject to the methodological weaknesses inherent in these methods (for a discussion, see Greene and Pennie 2015; Hemmerich and Ecker 2020), which means that, whenever possible, the results of QSAR models should be taken with caution and complemented with additional qualitative evidence. Third, I focused on inventions (by way of patents), but not all inventions become marketable products. Some countries – such as the EU member countries – have stringent procedures for screening toxic products, and the EU REACH regulation uses QSAR models to select out new chemical compounds if they are likely to be toxic based on extant knowledge. However, the regulations are less stringent elsewhere, and I know from prior research that some countries allow the use of highly toxic chemicals which are banned in other countries (Galt 2008). For instance, multinational companies operating in multiple global markets may exploit their knowledge and profiting from given toxic chemicals for as long as possible by taking advantage of some countries' lax regulatory environments.

References

Aghion, Philippe, Antoine Dechezleprêtre, David Hémous, Ralf Martin, and John Van Reenen. 2016. Carbon taxes, path dependency, and directed technical change: Evidence from the auto industry. *Journal of Political Economy* 124 (1): 1–51. https://doi.org/10.1086/684581.

Ahuja, Gautam, and Curba Morris Lampert. 2001. Entrepreneurship in the large corporation: A longitudinal study of how established firms create breakthrough inventions. *Strategic Management Journal* 22 (6–7): 521–543. https://doi.org/10.1002/smj.176.

Beggel, Sebastian, Inge Werner, Richard E. Connon, and Juergen P. Geist. 2010. Sublethal toxicity of commercial insecticide formulations and their active ingredients to larval fathead minnow (Pimephales promelas). *The Science of the Total Environment* 408 (16): 3169–3175. https://doi.org/10.1016/j.scitotenv.2010.04.004.

Bekkers, Rudi, Arianna Martinelli, and Federico Tamagni. 2020. The impact of including standards-related documentation in patent prior art: Evidence from an EPO policy change. *Research Policy* 49 (7): 104007. https://doi.org/10.1016/j.respol.2020.104007.

Benfenati, Emilio, Alberto Manganaro, and Giuseppina C Gini. 2013. *VEGA-QSAR: AI inside a platform for predictive toxicology*. PAI@ AI* IA.

Cherkasov, A., E.N. Muratov, D. Fourches, A. Varnek, I.I. Baskin, M. Cronin, J. Dearden, P. Gramatica, Y.C. Martin, R. Todeschini, V. Consonni, V.E. Kuz'Min, R. Cramer, R. Benigni, C. Yang, J. Rathman, L. Terfloth, J. Gasteiger, A. Richard, and A. Tropsha. 2014. QSAR modeling: Where have you been? Where are you going to? *Journal of Medicinal Chemistry* 57 (12): 4977–5010. https://doi.org/10.1021/jm4004285.

EC. 2010. *Europe 2020: A strategy for smart, sustainable and inclusive growth: Communication from the commission*. Brussels: Publications Office of the European Union.

Fitzgerald, L., and D.S. Wikoff. 2014. Persistent organic pollutants. In *Encyclopedia of toxicology*, ed. Philip Wexler, 3rd ed., 820–825. Oxford: Academic Press.

Galt, Ryan E. 2008. Beyond the circle of poison: Significant shifts in the global pesticide complex, 1976–2008. *Global Environmental Change* 18 (4): 786–799. https://doi.org/10.1016/j.gloenvcha.2008.07.003.

Greene, Nigel, and William Pennie. 2015. Computational toxicology, friend or foe? *Toxicology Research* 4 (5): 1159–1172. https://doi.org/10.1039/c5tx00055f.

Hemmerich, Jennifer, and Gerhard F. Ecker. 2020. In silico toxicology: From structure–activity relationships towards deep learning and adverse outcome pathways. *WIREs Computational Molecular Science* 10 (4): e1475. https://doi.org/10.1002/wcms.1475.

Kodavanti, P.R.S., J.E. Royland, and K.R.S. Sambasiva Rao. 2014. Toxicology of persistent organic pollutants. In *Reference module in biomedical sciences*. Amsterdam: Elsevier.

Kuhn, Jeffrey M., and Neil C. Thompson. 2019. How to measure and draw causal inferences with patent scope. *International Journal of the Economics of Business* 26 (1): 5–38.

Ma, Jianmin, Hayley Hung, Chongguo Tian, and Roland Kallenborn. 2011. Revolatilization of persistent organic pollutants in the Arctic induced by climate change. *Nature Climate Change* 1 (5): 255.

Marco, Alan C., Joshua D. Sarnoff, and Charles A.W. deGrazia. 2019. Patent claims and patent scope. *Research Policy* 48 (9): 103790. https://doi.org/10.1016/j.respol.2019.04.014.

Monosson, Emily. 2005. Chemical mixtures: Considering the evolution of toxicology and chemical assessment. *Environmental Health Perspectives* 113 (4): 383–390. https://doi.org/10.1289/ehp.6987.

Nizzetto, Luca, Matthew Macleod, Katrine Borgå, Ana Cabrerizo, Jordi Dachs, Antonio Di Guardo, Davide Ghirardello, Kaj M. Hansen, Andrew Jarvis, Anders Lindroth, Bernard Ludwig, Donald Monteith, Judith A. Perlinger, Martin Scheringer, Luitgard Schwendenmann, Kirk T. Semple, Lukas Y. Wick, Gan Zhang, and Kevin C. Jones. 2010. Past, present, and future controls on levels of persistent organic pollutants in the global environment. *Environmental Science & Technology* 44 (17): 6526–6531. https://doi.org/10.1021/es100178f.

Papadatos, George, Mark Davies, Nathan Dedman, Jon Chambers, Anna Gaulton, James Siddle, Richard Koks, Sean A. Irvine, Joe Pettersson, and Nicko Goncharoff. 2016. SureChEMBL: A large-scale, chemically annotated patent document database. *Nucleic Acids Research* 44 (D1): D1220–D1228.

Rigét, Frank, Anders Bignert, Birgit Braune, Maria Dam, Rune Dietz, Marlene Evans, Norman Green, Helga Gunnlaugsdóttir, Katrin S. Hoydal, John Kucklick, Robert Letcher, Derek Muir, Stacy Schuur, Christian Sonne, Gary Stern, Gregg Tomy, Katrin Vorkamp, and Simon Wilson. 2019. Temporal trends of persistent organic pollutants in Arctic marine and freshwater biota. *Science of the Total Environment* 649: 99–110. https://doi.org/10.1016/j.scitotenv.2018.08.268.

Shapiro, Joseph S., and Reed Walker. 2018. Why is pollution from US manufacturing declining? The roles of environmental regulation, productivity, and trade. *American Economic Review* 108 (12): 3814–3854. https://doi.org/10.1257/aer.20151272.

Van Noorden, Richard. 2018. Software beats animal tests at predicting toxicity of chemicals. *Nature* 559 (7713): 163–164.

Wallace, A.D. 2012. Toxic endpoints in the study of human exposure to environmental chemicals. *Progress in Molecular Biology and Translational Science* 112: 89–115. https://doi.org/10.1016/b978-0-12-415813-9.00004-0.

Zimmerman, Julie B., Paul T. Anastas, Hanno C. Erythropel, and Walter Leitner. 2020. Designing for a green chemistry future. *Science* 367 (6476): 397–400. https://doi.org/10.1126/science.aay3060.

Appendix: Details on the Selected QSAR Models

Human Toxicity

In order to assess the human health toxicity of the molecules in our sample of POP-related patent application, I consider 5 toxic effects on humans by using 17 QSAR models. Details of the different types of human toxicity and their evaluation are explained in detail in the following sections.

Mutagenicity

Results from the Ames test are the first outcome considered to assess the possible mutagenicity of chemical substances (Benfenati 2012). The Ames test is a widely employed method that uses bacteria to test whether the chemical substance of interest can cause mutations in the DNA of the test organism (Mortelmans and Zeiger 2000). In this paper, to predict mutagenicity endpoint, I perform Ames test throughout five different QSAR models. First, I use a consensus model which is an assessment of the predictions of the available VEGA HUB mutagenicity models (CAESAR, SarPy, ISS and KNN). The consensus algorithm uses the information provided in the assessment of each single model's prediction as its weight, so that the final assessment will be more influenced by the single models that produced more reliable predictions (Ferrari and Gini 2010; Benigni and Bossa 2008; Manganelli et al. 2020). Predictions from single models are associated with three possible levels of reliabilities: low, moderate and high. The consensus algorithm gives toxicity estimations ('mutagen', 'suspect mutagen' or 'non-mutagen') based on these levels of reliabilities. Second, I use the CAESAR model which, in turn, is composed by two models: Model A, a trained support vector machine (SVM) classifier, and an additional Model B for false-negative removal based on structural

G. Biggi, *Industrial Dynamics and Firm Strategies in the Agrochemical Industry*,
SpringerBriefs in Economics, https://doi.org/10.1007/978-3-031-52689-3

alerts (SAs) matching. Model B works with two sets of SAs: the first one is related to mutagenicity activity, if no matching is found the second set is checked, and if some matches are found, the prediction is 'suspect mutagen'. Third, I use the SarPy model which consists of two sets of rules for mutagenicity (112 rules) and non-mutagenicity (93 rules). If at least one mutagenicity rule is matching with the given compound, a 'mutagen' prediction is given; if only one or more non-mutagenicity rule is matching, a 'non-mutagen' prediction is given; if no rules match with the given compound, a 'possible non-mutagen' prediction is given. Fourth, I use an ISS model which is based on a set of rules, taken from the study of Benigni and Bossa (2011) on mutagenicity. If at least one mutagenicity rule is matching with the given compound, a 'mutagen' prediction is given; otherwise, a 'non-mutagen' prediction is given. Fifth, I use a KNN model which performs the assessment based on a dataset of 5770 chemicals. This dataset has been made by Istituto di Ricerche Farmacologiche Mario Negri, merging experimental data from a benchmark dataset compiled by Hansen et al. (2009) and from a collection of data made available by the Japan Health Ministry within their Ames QSAR project.

Carcinogenicity

Among various toxicological endpoints of chemical substances, carcinogenicity is of great concern because of its serious effects on human health. The carcinogenic mechanism of chemicals may be due to their ability to damage the genome or disrupt cellular metabolic processes. Carcinogenic chemicals have conventionally been divided into two categories according to the presumed mode of action: genotoxic or non-genotoxic. Genotoxic modes of action involve genetic alterations caused by the chemical interacting directly with DNA to result in a change in the primary sequence of DNA. Conversely, non-genotoxic modes of action do not involve alterations in DNA but that may influence gene expression, altered cell-cell communication or other factors involved in the carcinogenic process. In this paper, to predict the carcinogenicity endpoints of chemical substances, I use six different QSAR models. First is the CESAR model, which is built as a counter propagation artificial neural network (CP ANN). The neural network output consists of two values labelled as positive and non-positive, both in the range (0;1) and with sum equal to 1; they represent how much the neuron in which the predicted compound falls belongs to the class of 'carcinogenic' or 'non-carcinogenic' compounds (Fjodorova and Novič 2014). Second is the ISS model, developed from the works of Benigni and Bossa (2008, 2011) which define a training set for the model composed by of 797 compounds. If at least one carcinogen rule is matching with the given compound, a 'carcinogen' prediction is given; otherwise, a 'non-carcinogen' prediction is given. Third, the ANTARES model which includes a collection of chemical rat carcinogenesis data (presence of carcinogenic effects in male or female rats) obtained from the CAESAR project database and the 'FDA 2009 SAR Carcinogenicity – SAR Structures' database. The CAESAR toxicity values originated from the distributed structure-searchable toxicity DSSTox database, which was built from the Lois Gold's carcinogenic potency database (CPDB). The Sarpy software has been used with a cross-validated procedure, ending with the extraction of a set of 127 rules (structural alerts) related to carcinogenic activity. If at least one rule is matching with the given compound, a 'carcinogen' prediction is given. Otherwise, a 'possible non-carcinogen' prediction is given. Fourth is the ISSCAN/CGX model which consists in a set of 43 rules (structural alerts) related to carcinogenic activity. If at least one rule is matching with the given compound, a 'carcinogen' prediction is given. Otherwise, a 'possible non-carcinogen' prediction is given.

Teratogenicity

Teratogenicity is a manifestation of developmental toxicity, representing a particular case of embryo/fetotoxicity, by the induction or the increase of the frequency of structural disorders in the progeny (Van Gelder et al. 2010). This includes embryotoxic/fetotoxic effects such as reduced body weight, growth and developmental retardation, organ toxicity, death, abortion, structural defects (teratogenic effects), functional effects, peri- and postnatal defects and impaired postnatal mental or physical development up to and including normal pubertal development (Cassano et al. 2010). In this paper, I predict teratogenicity endpoints by relying on two QSAR models. First, I rely on CESAR model which is based on a binary classification of US Food and Drug Administration (FDA) criteria (FDA categories A and B are considered as 'non-toxicant', categories C, D and X are considered toxicant). Second, I rely on Procter & Gamble model in which 25 categories of possible toxicant have been identified. The model implements these categories and tries to find an exact match between the given compound and any of the virtual compounds in the library. If a match is found, a prediction of 'toxicant' is given; otherwise, a 'non-toxicant' prediction is provided.

Steroidal Activity

Steroidal activity may pose significant threats to both human health and the health of the aquatic wildlife given the widespread occurrence of estrogenic endocrine-disrupting compounds (Jobling and Tyler 2006). In this paper, to predict steroidal activity of chemical substances, I rely on three QSAR models. First, oestrogen receptor relative binding affinity model which is a QSAR classification model based on a classification and regression tree (CART) algorithm (Roncaglioni et al. 2008) composed by a training set of the model, taken from the cited work, consists of 806 compounds. Second is oestrogen receptor-mediated effect model which is a classification model for endocrine disruptor screening. The model has been built as a set of rules, extracted with Sarpy software from a dataset obtained from a collection of high-quality oestrogen receptor (ER) signalling data (1529 chemicals screened across 18 high-throughput screening assays integrated into a single score). The Sarpy software has been used with a cross-validated procedure, ending with the extraction of two sets of rules (structural alerts) related to ER-mediated effect activity and inactivity (for a total of 59 rules). These rules have been further divided, according to their statistical significance, into a subset of rules with strong statistical evidence and another one of rules with weaker evidence. These rules are expressed SMARTS representing molecular fragments. If at least one rule for activity is matching with the given compound, an 'active' or 'possible active' prediction is given, depending on the statistical evidence of the rule. If no active rules are found, but at least one rule for non-activity is matching with the given compound, a 'non-active' or 'possible non-active' prediction is given, depending on the statistical evidence of the rule. If no rules are matching at all, no prediction is provided.

Liver Damage

The liver plays a central role in toxicology. It is the primary organ of detoxification and elimination by metabolism of many chemicals. The term 'hepatotoxicity' means chemical-driven liver damage. Indeed, chemical substances, such as those used in agriculture and industry, as well as organic chemicals may induce hepatotoxicity. In this paper, to predict liver damage endpoints, I consider the hepatotoxicity model developed by IRFMN which provides a qualitative prediction of hepatotoxicity (drug-induced liver injury). The model is composed by a set of rules, both extracted with Sarpy software and manually created by expert from a data set of 950 compounds using data from the literature and further tested on an external validation set of 101 compounds. The development of the model is reported in Pizzo and Benfenati (2016). If at least one rule is matching with the given compound, a prediction is given; otherwise, the model reports a 'unknown' activity prediction. When one or more rules are matching, if the number of rules related to toxicity is higher or equal than the number of rules for nontoxicity, a 'toxic' prediction is provided; otherwise, a 'non-toxic' prediction is provided.

Environmental Toxicity

In order to assess the environmental toxicity of the molecules in our sample of POPs-related patent application, I consider five environmental hazards using five QSAR models. Details of the different types of environmental toxicity and their evaluation are explained in detail in the following sections.

Fish Acute Toxicity

Fish acute (LC50) toxicity classification provides a qualitative evaluation divided in four toxicity classes of fish toxicity. The model is built as three sets of rules, related to different toxicity classes. Each of the three set contains a list of relevant fragments related to the first three toxicity classes, defined on the basis of the classification for toxicity to fish provided by Directive 92/32/EEC of the EU for dangerous substances and listed in Table A1.

If one or more rules are verified for the given compound, the model will assign the compound to the most toxic class available among the verified rules. If no rules apply to the given compound, the prediction will be class 4. The extraction of the rules has been performed on a training set consisting of 567 compounds, where experimental data, originally expressed as acute toxicity database to fathead minnow (*Pimephales promelas*), has been classified on the basis of the reported scheme.

Algae Toxicity

Algae classification toxicity model provides a classification model for toxicity in algae (*Pseudokirchneriella subcapitata*), specific for biocides. It has been developed inside the EU LIFE COMBASE project (LIFE15 ENV/ES/416). A biocide-like chemical space was developed comparing 6512 chemical structures from the Physprop database and 257 chemical structures of biocides from COMBASE database. Five molecular descriptors were selected as filters. These filters were applied to the Japanese Ministry of Environment dataset for acute aquatic toxicity in algae (650 compounds), and finally I obtained a dataset of 361 biocide-like structures. The qualitative model has been developed using the automated neural networks (ANN) analysis and based on the 361 filtered compounds. The compounds were randomly distributed in training set (254), test set (53) and external validation set (54). The descriptors used in this model are the following: 'toxic' or 'non-toxic'.

Table A1 Fish toxicity classes

Class	LC50	Damage
1	<1 mg/L	Very toxic to aquatic organisms
2	1–10 mg/L	Toxic to aquatic organisms
3	10–100 mg/L	Harmful to aquatic organisms
4	>100 mg/L	May cause long term adverse effects to aquatic organisms

Bee Acute Toxicity

The bee acute toxicity model provides a qualitative evaluation, divided in three toxicity classes, for acute contact toxicity in honeybees (*Apis mellifera*). The model is based on a set of 256 compounds with known experimental toxicity data. The dataset contains experimental data binned in three toxicity classes: 'strong toxicity', 'moderate toxicity' and 'low toxicity'. This model is based on the similarity index developed inside the VEGA HUB platform; the index takes into account several structural aspects of the compounds, such as their fingerprint and the number of atoms, cycles, heteroatoms, halogen atoms and particular fragments (such as nitro groups). The index value ranges from 1 (maximum similarity) to 0. On the basis of this structural similarity index, the four compounds from the dataset resulting most similar to the chemical to be predicted are taken into account; compounds with a similarity value lower than 0.7 are discarded, and if only one compound remains available for prediction, it is kept only if it has a similarity value higher than 0.75. If no compounds fall under these conditions, no prediction is provided. The prediction is calculated as the most representative class in the compound selected with the above-mentioned procedure, considering their similarity index values as a weight so that the most similar compounds have a higher influence in the prediction.

Sludge Toxicity

The Sludge Classification Toxicity model takes into account 6.512 chemical structures from the Physprop database and 257 chemical structures of biocides from COMBASE database. Five molecular descriptors were selected as filters. These filters were applied to the experimental data found within the different databases from the QSAR Toolbox V 4.2 (https://qsartoolbox.org/). First, 94 biocide-like compounds were found by application of the biocide-chemical space and were used to develop the qualitative model settling the cutoff to discriminate between a 'toxic' and a 'non-toxic' compound in 100 mg/L. The whole dataset was divided into training and validation set randomly, and a classification using Boosted Trees analysis was used for the model development.

Ready Biodegradability

The ready biodegradability model is based on the OECD TG 301C-modified MITI-I test data and provides a qualitative evaluation (binary classification) of ready biodegradability properties. The model has been built as a set of rules, extracted from the training set with Sarpy software. The final set of fragments obtained come from a work that involved both a statistical part and an expert-based part. Seven different rule-sets of fragments related to ready biodegradability activity were obtained: rule-set 1 (non-readily biodegradable fragments with high specificity), rule-set 2 (non-readily biodegradable fragments with balanced performance), rule-set 3 (readily biodegradable fragments with high specificity), rule-set 4 (readily biodegradable fragments with balanced performance), rule-set 5 (readily biodegradable fragments extracted from unknown), rule-set 6 (non-readily biodegradable expert-based fragments) and rule-set 7 (ready biodegradable expert-based fragments). The overall model is conservative, and in case of the presence of conflicting fragments, the prediction is for 'non-readily biodegradability'. The logical scheme of the model comes directly from a chemical reasoning: a substance is always considered 'non-biodegradable' if at least one fragment related to non-biodegradability is found, even if easily biodegradable fragments are found; this means that a part of the compound is anyway persistent.

References

Benfenati, Emilio. 2012. *Theory, guidance and applications on QSAR and REACH*. E-book available at: http://www.orchestra-qsar.eu/documents/333.

Benigni, R., and C. Bossa. 2008. Structure alerts for carcinogenicity, and the Salmonella assay system: A novel insight through the chemical relational databases technology. *Mutation Research* 659 (3): 248–261. https://doi.org/10.1016/j.mrrev.2008.05.003.

———. 2011. Mechanisms of chemical carcinogenicity and mutagenicity: A review with implications for predictive toxicology. *Chemical Reviews* 111 (4): 2507–2536. https://doi.org/10.1021/cr100222q.

Cassano, Antonio, Alberto Manganaro, Todd Martin, Douglas Young, Nadège Piclin, Marco Pintore, Davide Bigoni, and Emilio Benfenati. 2010. CAESAR models for developmental toxicity. *Chemistry Central Journal* 4 (Suppl 1): S4–S4. https://doi.org/10.1186/1752-153X-4-S1-S4.

Ferrari, Thomas, and Giuseppina Gini. 2010. An open source multistep model to predict mutagenicity from statistical analysis and relevant structural alerts. *Chemistry Central Journal* 4 (1): S2. https://doi.org/10.1186/1752-153X-4-S1-S2.

Fjodorova, N., and M. Novič. 2014. Comparison of criteria used to access carcinogenicity in CPANN QSAR models versus the knowledge-based expert system Toxtree. *SAR and QSAR in Environmental Research* 25 (6): 423–441. https://doi.org/10.1080/1062936x.2014.898687.

Hansen, Katja, Sebastian Mika, Timon Schroeter, Andreas Sutter, Antonius Ter Laak, Thomas Steger-Hartmann, Nikolaus Heinrich, and Klaus-Robert Müller. 2009. Benchmark data set for in silico prediction of Ames mutagenicity. *Journal of Chemical Information and Modeling* 49 (9): 2077–2081.

Jobling, Susan, and Charles R. Tyler. 2006. Introduction: The ecological relevance of chemically induced endocrine disruption in wildlife. *Environmental Health Perspectives* 114 (Suppl 1): 7–8. https://doi.org/10.1289/ehp.8046.

Manganelli, Serena, Benoît Schilter, Gabriele Scholz, Emilio Benfenati, and Elena Lo Piparo. 2020. Value and limitation of structure-based profilers to characterize developmental and reproductive toxicity potential. *Archives of Toxicology* 94 (3): 939–954. https://doi.org/10.1007/s00204-020-02671-z.

Mortelmans, K., and E. Zeiger. 2000. The Ames Salmonella/microsome mutagenicity assay. *Mutation Research* 455 (1–2): 29–60. https://doi.org/10.1016/s0027-5107(00)00064-6.

Pizzo, F., and E. Benfenati. (2016). In silico models for repeated-dose toxicity (RDT): Prediction of the no observed adverse effect level (NOAEL) and lowest observed adverse effect level (LOAEL) for drugs. In silico methods for predicting drug toxicity, 163–176.

G. Biggi, *Industrial Dynamics and Firm Strategies in the Agrochemical Industry*, SpringerBriefs in Economics, https://doi.org/10.1007/978-3-031-52689-3

Roncaglioni, A., N. Piclin, M. Pintore, and E. Benfenati. 2008. Binary classification models for endocrine disrupter effects mediated through the estrogen receptor. *SAR and QSAR in Environmental Research* 19 (7-8): 697–733. https://doi.org/10.1080/10629360802550606.

Van Gelder, Marleen M.H.J., Iris A.L.M. Van Rooij, Richard K. Miller, Gerhard A. Zielhuis, Lolkje T.W. de Jong-van den Berg, and Nel Roeleveld. 2010. Teratogenic mechanisms of medical drugs. *Human Reproduction Update* 16 (4): 378–394.

GPSR Compliance
The European Union's (EU) General Product Safety Regulation (GPSR) is a set of rules that requires consumer products to be safe and our obligations to ensure this.

If you have any concerns about our products, you can contact us on

ProductSafety@springernature.com

In case Publisher is established outside the EU, the EU authorized representative is:

Springer Nature Customer Service Center GmbH
Europaplatz 3
69115 Heidelberg, Germany

www.ingramcontent.com/pod-product-compliance
Ingram Content Group UK Ltd.
Pitfield, Milton Keynes, MK11 3LW, UK
UKHW020151290926
15471UKWH00004B/803
* 9 7 8 3 0 3 1 5 2 6 8 8 6 *